Strategic Communication and AI

This concise text provides an accessible introduction to artificial intelligence and intelligent user interfaces (IUIs) and how they are at the heart of a communication revolution for strategic communications and public relations.

IUIs are where users and technology meet – via computers, phones, robots, public displays, etc. They use AI and machine learning methods to control how those systems interact, exchange data, learn from, and develop relations with users. The authors explore research and developments that are already changing human/machine engagement in a wide range of areas from consumer goods, healthcare, and entertainment to community relations, crisis management, and activism. They also explore the implications for public relations of how technologies developing hyper-personalised persuasion could be used to make choices for us, navigating the controversial space between influence, nudging, and controlling.

This readable overview of the applications and implications of AI and IUIs will be welcomed by researchers, students, and practitioners in all areas of strategic communication, public relations, and communications studies.

Simon Moore is Associate Professor in the Department of Information Design & Corporate Communication at Bentley University in Massachusetts, USA.

Roland Hübscher is Associate Professor in the Department of Information Design & Corporate Communication at Bentley University in Massachusetts, USA.

Routledge Insights in Public Relations Research

The field of PR research has grown exponentially in recent years and academics at all career levels are seeking authoritative publication opportunities for their scholarship. **Routledge Insights in Public Relations Research** is a new program of short-form book publications, presenting key topics across the discipline and their foundation in research. This series will provide a forward-facing global forum for new and emerging research topics which critically evaluate contemporary PR thinking and practice.

This format is particularly effective for introducing new scholarship reflecting the diverse range of research approaches and topics in the field. It is particularly effective for:

- Overview of an emerging area or "hot topic".
- In-depth case-study.
- Tailored research-based information for a practitioner readership.
- Update of a research paper to reflect new findings or wider perspectives.
- Exploration of analytical or theoretical innovations.
- Topical response to current affairs or policy debates.

Authors from practice and the academy will be able to quickly pass on their thinking and findings to fellow PR scholars, researchers, MA and PhD students and informed practitioners.

Strategic Communication and AI
Public Relations with Intelligent User Interfaces
Simon Moore and Roland Hübscher

For more information about this series, please visit: www.routledge.com/ Routledge-Insights-in-Public-Relations-Research/book-series/RIPRR

Strategic Communication and AI
Public Relations with Intelligent User Interfaces

Simon Moore and
Roland Hübscher

Routledge
Taylor & Francis Group

LONDON AND NEW YORK

First published 2022
by Routledge
2 Park Square, Milton Park, Abingdon, Oxon OX14 4RN

and by Routledge
605 Third Avenue, New York, NY 10158

Routledge is an imprint of the Taylor & Francis Group, an informa business

© 2022 Simon Moore and Roland Hübscher

The right of Simon Moore and Roland Hübscher to be identified as authors of this work has been asserted by them in accordance with sections 77 and 78 of the Copyright, Designs and Patents Act 1988.

British Library Cataloguing-in-Publication Data
A catalogue record for this book is available from the British Library

Library of Congress Cataloging-in-Publication Data
Names: Moore, Simon, 1961– author. | Hübscher, Roland, 1961– author.
Title: Strategic communication and AI : public relations with intelligent user interfaces / Simon Moore and Roland Hübscher.
Description: Abingdon, Oxon ; New York, NY : Routledge, 2022. |
Series: Routledge insights in public relations research |
Includes bibliographical references and index.
Identifiers: LCCN 2021027074 (print) |
LCCN 2021027075 (ebook)
Subjects: LCSH: Public relations—Technological innovations. | Communication—Technological innovations. | User interfaces (Computer systems) | Artificial intelligence—Marketing applications.
Classification: LCC HM1221 .M668 2022 (print) |
LCC HM1221 (ebook) | DDC 659.2—dc23
LC record available at https://lccn.loc.gov/2021027074
LC ebook record available at https://lccn.loc.gov/2021027075

ISBN: 978-0-367-62779-9 (hbk)
ISBN: 978-0-367-62896-3 (pbk)
ISBN: 978-1-003-11132-0 (ebk)

DOI: 10.4324/9781003111320

Typeset in Times New Roman
by codeMantra

To my aunts, Frances Watson and Sheila Greenman.
With love.
SM

To my wife Teresa and daughter Sophia. Thank you for
your patience.
RH

Contents

Acknowledgements

We would like to thank Erik Austin, Bentley University's Department of Information Design & Corporate Communication, Bentley University Library and its many databases, Pierre Berthon, Don Bobiash, Ian Cross, Sandra den Otter, Jon Ericsson, Bill Gribbons, Bernie Kavanagh, Rahul Kumar, Ruth MacSween, Graeme Mew, Mike Michielin, Sophie, Imogen and Isobel Moore, Jim Pouliopolous, Cliff Putney, our reviewers, the Routledge team, Theresa Rozkiewicz, Javed Siddiqi, Mike Tesler, Andrew Tietzen, Mounia Ziat.

Abbreviations

AA	Artificial agent
AI	Artificial intelligence
AR	Augmented reality
B2i	Business to individual
BCI	Brain computer interaction
DPA	Digital personal assistant
HCI	Human computer interaction
CUI	Conversational user interface
GUI	Graphical user interface
IUI	Intelligent user interface
M2M	Machine to machine
PR	Public relations
PUI	Persuasive user interface
VUI	Voice user interface
UX	User experience
VE	Virtual environments
VR	Virtual reality

1 Intelligent user interfaces (IUIs)

The next generation of digital communication

Reasons for this book

'We believe that user interface design is poised for a radical change in the near future', wrote the authors of a research paper published in 2000 (Boyd et al., 1990, p. 24). Over 20 years later, public relations (PR) still has much to discover about interfaces. This will soon change thanks to a combination of real-world events and, hopefully, closer study: PR is about to witness and work with the next generation of interfaces, intelligent user interfaces (IUIs or just 'interfaces' in this book).

People and electronic devices interact and communicate via a user interface through mouse or hand gestures, speech, smell, touch, or even the emotions we show with our faces and body. We are still mainly living in a world dominated by graphical user interfaces (GUIs) developed back in the 1960s by Doug Engelbart and then at Xerox PARC. But a new kind of interface has begun to go beyond this limiting direct-manipulation form of interaction. Using artificial intelligence (AI) methods, IUIs adapt to the user's interests, recommend what to buy or listen to, sense the stress level in city traffic, or help cut through the enormous amount of, mostly useless, information we are bombarded with. How people interact and communicate with such IUIs is qualitatively different from interacting with GUIs. IUIs are especially useful because they allow the machine to interpret what the users mean and don't just have to take them literally, as is the case now with the routine of click on this button or press that key. PR will need to adapt and take advantage of the enormous potential IUIs present.

From PR's perspective, user interfaces are 'where bits and people meet' (Negroponte, 1996, p. 87; Jaquero et al., 2009, p. 260). They help machines like phones and other devices that are mobile, wearable, or fixed in place find out what people want or believe. They help us find

DOI: 10.4324/9781003111320-1

out what organisations want or believe, working through an interface that appeals to one or more human senses. The coming generation of interfaces, deploying AI, will have advanced communication powers and for that reason will become essential to PR (also known as strategic communication, a term now being adopted by industry and scholarship).

Interfaces and PR already have several things in common. Like PR practitioners, in fact like most if not all of us, IUIs often treat data with some bias. Data and persuasion matter to IUIs as they do to PR which also goes where bits, people, and organisations meet. PR and IUIs can encourage two-way communication, create or adjudicate power relations, and shape action by shaping perceptions.

It's been pointed out that 'The economy of bits is driven in part by the constraints of the medium on which it is stored and through which it is delivered' (Negroponte, 1996, p. 14). The economy of PR is constrained the same way, and like bits (the units of information in digital communications) PR is experiencing fewer limits; there are more ways for PR to deliver a message, invoke a feeling, and shape a decision. This book asks what sort of IUIs could work with PR, and the effect of that partnership on the organisation and the target audience.

To deliver a message effectively, organisations must encourage us to connect with a media platform, and to trust it. They want us to find its media platforms attractive, helpful, authoritative, powerful, perhaps addictive, or at least acceptable and trustworthy. All media platforms are interfaces, and the tale of our attraction to interfaces from cave walls to mobile phones is repeated with the IUI: its design and construction, its appeal to our senses and to our reason through our senses. Interfaces tell a story about the groups trying to speak to us.

Frustrated by incomplete or unsatisfying data, we might prefer messages that an IUI can express better than existing media. IUIs might build more satisfying relationships with us or destroy carefully built trust. Thanks to machine learning, an IUI may learn how to be our friend or pretend to be our friend in order to deceive us, and how to uncouple our interior world from conventions and standards held by those close to us, or alternatively how to reinforce those connections if it helps the organisation's PR goals. Depending on what we think of the organisation using the IUI for PR, interfaces could liberate or isolate us from peer pressure or peer protection. The IUI may show us new ways to experience and welcome messages crafted by people we have never met and do not really know.

At a basic level, an IUI is as 'invisible' as PR can be. It could function almost unnoticed. Until it goes wrong, it might be quite unobtrusive when we talk with a customer relations associate or a government official, place an order, read an e-book, but two sides are still encountering one another through it. Unobtrusive or not, the outcome of that encounter may depend in part on the interface design, the subject it communicates, the existing relations between the two sides, and the urgency or importance of the interchange.

PR will be concerned with how a user will accept, like, or trust the IUI. It is possible that some IUIs will be capable of convincingly informal communication conventions, and use them to make an organisation more 'likeable'. Building a personal relationship using planned communication is hardly a new process, but IUIs could intensify its impact. Communication between organisations and audiences already seems much more personal, thanks to our inability to resist the many and varied screens that fill modern life. The situation was foreshadowed in E.M. Forster's dystopic novella *The Machine Stops*, written in 1909 and which still repays reading. Our book looks at this process again and asks why IUIs will be at the heart of another communication realignment between humans, machines, and organisations. Running throughout the book is the belief that PR must now understand IUIs in their own right, and not mistake them as design features of the technology they are attached to.

IUIs have some way to go as fully realised PR assets. In their current stage of development, they are already becoming a useful way for us to obtain goods and health or educational services, but only to a limited, volatile, and erratic extent with ideas, reputations, or opinions. In spite of that, IUIs are already influencing reputations as they channel the personalities of the device and of the organisation communicating through it, and manage the information exchange with human users. On top of that, IUIs already want us to *learn* things, or cooperate in practical tasks. PR will use them to persuade us to *believe* things about companies, products, governments at all levels and of all political stripes, about campaign groups, communities, global nonprofits, and other kinds of organisations.

IUIs are rapidly learning the arts of persuasion, and to nudge, to sympathise, to encourage, to scrutinise, to play. They exemplify a tendency described in 1964 by the Canadian scholar of communication Marshal McLuhan (1911–1980). By extending ourselves into electric media he wrote, in *Understanding media: the extensions of* man, 'we have extended our central nervous system itself in a global embrace':

> Whether the extension of consciousness, so long sought by advertisers for specific products, will be 'a good thing' is a question that admits of a wide solution.
>
> (McLuhan & Gordon, 2013, Introduction)

Viewed as a machine with mechanical innards, IUIs are neither good nor bad and some of us will approach them cautiously, and only extend ourselves through IUIs because everyone else is doing it, leaving the sceptics with no choice. Paraphrasing a bank robber's celebrated justification that banks are where the money is, IUIs will be where the information is, and we'll have to go to them to get it.

Whatever our misgivings, however, McLuhan was surely right to say that 'Any extension, whether of skin, hand or foot, affects the whole psychic and social complex' (McLuhan & Gordon, 2013, Introduction). We discover new media the same way an infant discovers its limbs, with the same wonder and curiosity, the same thrill at its new powers. IUIs, once PR discovers them, will arouse the same sense of excitement and novelty, and the urge to play and experiment.

This book asks why, how, and what kinds of IUIs might be harnessed by PR practitioners who will also have to deal with IUIs as the audience since interfaces listen to news or marketing information, and interpret and filter them. It believes with McLuhan that 'the need to understand the effects of the extensions of man becomes more urgent by the hour' (Introduction). IUIs will be the latest test of our technological maturity, our ability to live with the tools we have created. The more we come to rely on them, the more IUIs will wield a power of their own, using it to extend themselves just as we use media to extend ourselves and escape the limits of our biology.

We try to look at IUIs through the eyes of someone interested in PR. We ask if IUIs – guided by PR's needs – could ultimately make many choices for us, operating in the debatable space between persuasion, nudging, and commanding, partly by mastering communication skills once limited to human beings. What choices would interfaces make? Could McLuhan's dictum 'the media is the message' eventually become 'the media is the mind'?

What kinds of IUIs are there?

If history is any guide, IUIs used as media platforms will start as tools to help PR say what it largely would have said anyway. Slowly or quickly, IUIs will then become interpreters and then arbiters of content, choices, and identities because they will be the faces of organisations. Which interfaces in development today will bring us to this point? Difficult to say: perhaps the cousins of projects underway at the Future Interfaces Group (FIG) at Carnegie Mellon University in the USA. All of them are essentially, as McLuhan prognosticated, extensions of a user's nervous system, to the point of 'Appropriating the human body as an interactive surface', in the words of a FIG team investigating 'on-skin touch interfaces' (Xiao et al., 2018, p. 1). Appropriating previously mute objects is being investigated as well. 'Direct', another FIG interface, is a touch-tracking algorithm to turn any flat surface into 'an ad-hoc, touch-sensitive display' (Xiao et al., 2016, p. 1), by effectively measuring the user's touch and (distance) to the surface.

The value of an algorithm like Direct to PR isn't limited to the information swapped between audiences and organisations. It is the ability to make any surface interactive. 'Direct' and projects like it make a connection between human and medium that supplements or surpasses other connections between humans and organisations, and sometimes between humans. Touch-tracking algorithms like Direct might admit more organisations more closely into our lives by embedding them into whatever we, not they, decide is media: tables, walls, appliances. They are part of an oft-predicted future that foresees an Internet of things: interfaces everywhere and anywhere we want, creating a false impression that we're communicating with an organisation on our terms, in our space, not seeing that we have turned our own space over to someone else's interface.

In these senses, IUIs could smooth encounters between organisation and human. IUIs ideally want to understand what humans undertake or think, our whole environment for perceiving, deciding, and acting. It is possible that their curiosity may improve our ability to be intelligent and creative beings. A lot of research asks how IUIs can boost our creativity or help people with cognitive or physical challenges – perhaps by playing games or by more formal education – or in the title of an early paper act as 'An expert system that volunteers advice' (Shrager & Finin, 1982).

Words like 'education' and 'intelligent' must be refined to see what they mean for IUIs that could work for PR practitioners. This book thinks about the kind of intelligence IUIs need to be useful to PR, and asks what an IUI's ability to educate and persuade means for PR, beyond enabling a straight two-way data exchange between the IUI and the human user – that adaptable, malleable, organic 'U' in a technological sandwich of 'Intelligent' and 'Interface'.

The following chapters see IUIs the way PR will want to see them. IUIs must be capable of watching and touching, understanding and feeling, choosing and acting, helping and persuading, listening and learning, managing and controlling. IUIs could engage the human senses far more intensively than existing media. Perhaps in PR's hands, they will have the same revolutionary spiritualised impact as the first cave paintings. Could they affect PR to the point of changing its assumptions about operational strategy and human nature, or must IUIs conform to the fundamental principles that have always guided PR?

What could IUIs do to PR?

Hyper-personalisation

It is not enough to reduce the implications of IUIs for PR to a description of its features plus a paragraph on ethical implications. It is in fact reckless to treat IUIs as the technical sum of their parts. The agents of persuasion affect us morally as well as materially, and perhaps biologically as well. What does the advent of PR-mediated IUIs mean for society?

Because the interface can feel more personal, as we suggested earlier, IUIs might strengthen many of PR's existing functions: joining audiences to organisations, delivering messages, gathering opinion and data, encouraging particular choices. A user interacting with an IUI through a Brain-Computer Interface could feel a far closer connection with the organisation. An organisation or person can rapidly adjust an IUI-mediated experience towards or away from particular expectations, discover or create new audience identities, perhaps co-create a message with its target audiences, even as it is being communicated in words, sounds, touch, or images. IUIs, we shall see, could capture and contain the processes of designing a PR message, experiencing a PR activity and acting on it, without altogether abolishing them as separate functions.

IUIs are the latest stage in a social development characterised by techniques and media for persuasion, not orders; and if not persuasion, a 'soft' compulsion diluted with the language of persuasion. Because of this ability to 'nudge' and their ability to make communication more personal, IUIs could grow the identities that matter to individuals seeking to connect with organisations. This could be to the good. The complex needs of public communication have already widened the choices, identities, and ideas available to us. It has brought more people into the public sphere, and their preferred subjects and needs. PR has helped keep us as a 'public' important to society. Perhaps in time, IUIs will lead this development as a distinct form of PR, since 'The IUI objectives are to increase productivity, decrease expenditures, and improve efficiency, effectiveness, and naturalness of interaction' (Sonntag, 2017, pp. 1–2). A 2019 patent application for chatbots 'aims to make it easier for users to interact with the companies and accomplish their desired actions' (Microsoft, 2019). PR will be attracted to the potential of interfaces for, among many other fields, community relations, employee engagement, celebrity publicity, crisis communication, corporate social responsibility, investor relations, is- sues management, public affairs campaigning, government relations, healthcare communication, sports PR, and events PR.

We noted an early definition of user interfaces as expert systems that proactively volunteer advice (see above, Shrager & Finin, 1982). To 'volunteer' advice needs a medium that can review available options, make a choice, and decide the best way to suggest it. IUIs move us to- wards the idea of 'Computers as persuasive social actors' (Fogg, 2003, p. 89); first, because persuasion in a public sphere will matter as long as organisations and machines continue to value human cooperation. Cooperation requires persuasion; making a case not giving orders. Persuasion on a tremendous scale requires strategic communication. The second reason is our already-mentioned attraction to inanimate objects. We often find technology or other items compelling, silently persuasive. Marx called it 'the fetishism of the commodity' in volume 1 of *Capital*, and made it a plank in his political critique (Marx et al., 1990, p. 163). In recent times:

The fact that people respond socially to computer products has significant implications for persuasion. It opens the door for com- puters to apply a host of persuasion dynamics that are collectively described as social influence.

(Fogg, 2003, p. 90)

The idea of turning walls, or any other flat surface of our own homes (showers? Doors?) into a persuasive agent may produce mixed feelings, which are often defeated by that fascination with inorganic objects that seem to want a relationship with us, a magical fascination we have known since childhood. This leaves PR with the task of discovering what might be useful from among IUI's 'host of persuasion dynamics'. This book tries to show where PR should look, and the implications for PR and society. The founder of Stanford University's Behavior Design Lab wrote of 'mass interpersonal persuasion' (MIP) powered by technology that:

brings together the power of interpersonal persuasion with the reach of mass media. I believe this new way to change attitudes and behavior is the most significant advance in persuasion since radio was invented in the 1890s.

(Fogg, 2008, p. 23)

Society is starting to immerse itself in that world, accepting or resisting the changes it is making to the way we process information, reason, feel, and choose, depending on what we think of the organisation doing the communicating. There will be hiccups. Occasionally we will pause and worry about the consequences depending on who the communicator is at a given moment. At other times, as often happens now, we'll have no objections at all – especially if we agree with the communicator. Whatever the doubts though, PR can't ignore this new hyper-personalised persuasive atmosphere. It is too risky to ignore. For one thing, individuals might prefer to communicate with IUIs quite naturally and spontaneously, as we do with each other. Organisations trying to navigate a revolution in spontaneity will need PR to help them.

Audiences: from the 'mass' to the 'individual'

PR is traditionally interested in groups, masses, and audiences. In 1928, PR pioneer Edward Bernays advocated the 'systematic study of mass psychology' to reveal 'the potentialities of invisible government' which was his view of what PR was (Bernays, 2005, p. 71). Another well-known PR contemporary, Ivy Ledbetter Lee, looked forward to the 'yet newer and better technique of appealing to mass psychology' (Lee, 1934, p. 23). PR wants to understand the individual's connection to the mass, because industrial-era communication messages could only be delivered by connecting to the individual's membership of a particular 'mass' which already existed or which the communicators could summon into existence to receive specific messages and take specific actions, as consumers or in other aspects of life.

Even without IUIs, a change in PR's view of the mass (whether of people or opinion or action) is underway. The information revolution is crumbling the mass into ever-smaller units. The 'mass' in 'mass interpersonal persuasion' works in the mathematical sense of an individual with the potential to reach very many other individuals. In a PR sense, the phrase becomes less useful when we think about IUIs, because IUIs will design an intensely individual process, in which the organisation has a humanlike personality, which can connect with our individuality far more intimately than almost any media in history. The following pages show how it might happen. Managed as a PR asset, IUIs will adjust to whichever of our many identities seem most helpful. PR will operate in a less stable arena. The older PR and propaganda methods that we react to as a 'mass', and ideas of society as a series of 'groups' to be activated or side-lined as required, may shift into fluid personal preferences that might briefly align with others, before dissolving once commercial or civic needs are satisfied or defeated.

It is justifiable to ask what a PR–IUI partnership might mean for honest communication or independent opinion-forming. In 2019, research in financial services concluded that humans gave 'conversational robo advisors'' 'greater levels of affective trust' compared to their non-conversational counterparts, which influenced perceptions of the financial services company, 'which can lead to detrimental consequences for consumers' like choosing inappropriate and expensive recommendations (Hildebrand & Bergner, 2019, p. 123). Human advisors presumably are capable of doing the same thing, and robo advisors might make good recommendations as well. Persuasion dynamics and opinion formation are popular topics in human-computer interaction and social media, and the scale of this research makes it likely that IUIs will get better at persuasion. A social media study reminded its readers that 'Opinion formation is a complex process involving individual mentality and group behavior' (Yin et al., 2019, p. 560). This is unlikely to discourage IUI designers but the changing conditions for public communication suggests their work might in the end put more weight on individual mentality than group behaviours.

IUIs then may make PR's messages into something more than a message, by taking the 'mass' out of media and 'altering the posture and relations of our senses', according to McLuhan, who tested that principle when investigating any widely adopted new media (McLuhan & Gordon, 2011, p. 55). If IUIs are bound by the same principle, they could convert PR into an activity concerned with understanding the individual as an individual. IUI-driven PR could, in short, take more interest in the qualities of the individual mind than in the character of a collective identity. More impetus may come from the idea of 'B2i' – Business to Individual marketing and communication. IUIs may in turn fuel B2i which has, probably wrongly, been called '"the last mile" of digital transformation' (PR Week, 2021) as the means of achieving a much more personal connection between individuals and organisations.

The message: from 'command' to 'cloud'

Messages are the binding agents of PR strategy. For a target audience, a message can feel subjective or objective, can be a subject or a physical object to be transmitted in ways that best connect with the people who need to receive it. A message can be contained in an appeal to any or (better still) all of the human senses, the biological interfaces between our external and internal lives. However mundane the message is, it reflects human psychology, history, and other expressions of our intellect. Seen at a distance though the delivery process is quite mechanical, and in PR appears to follow principles identified by the mathematician Claude Shannon in 'A Mathematical Theory of Communication' published in 1948, later written into a book with Warren Weaver. The theory originated in an attempt to understand the process of encoding electronic messages, but the model eventually became important to evolutionary biology, information theory, and public relations. Like electronic communication, these fields need a communication system that consists of an information source, a transmitter to interpret it and who 'operates on the message', a channel to transmit signals, something to receive and reconstruct the message, and a destination for whom the message is intended (Shannon, 1948, pp. 380–381). Shannon's theory was a clever attempt to break down a complex process, and its connection to PR's activities is immediately clear. It is the essence of the process PR oversees.

Will that remain the case in a world of IUIs? What happens to message formation and delivery, and to older theories that tried to bottle that process? Technology advances usually affect the speed and volume of messages, make more complex communication possible, and create more diverse functions for PR to manage as human knowledge and skills become more specialised. IUIs may be different. They don't look likely at present to significantly increase the speed or timing of messages. In PR, speed is already virtually instantaneous if required, and PR's messages on behalf of organisations often play with timing. IUIs may not change the quantity of PR messages either; that has already been increased by existing channels transmitting to the 'something' that receives and perceives them, and sends responses back to the source. The effect of IUIs will be different and mainly based on their impact on our reason and imagination. They will use technology to reconstruct existing messages in new and compelling ways, ways better at encouraging the minds at the destination to receive them, perhaps adjust them, enrich them, and co-own them using IUIs of their own. IUIs, therefore, will not change PR's dependence on Shannon's theory. They do raise the prospect that we as receivers will have our own computation agent at work in the public sphere: collecting, categorising, filtering and summarising, and presenting the information for us.

We shall see why more people using more interfaces to persuade does not mean the end of public relations. Organisations will still need people who can communicate to other people on their behalf and understand the media that delivers and influences the communication.

IUIs actually reinforce PR's need to oversee a consistent, coordinated message, a message presented as an idea and that through closer engagement with our senses could become less absolute, less definitive, and more of a cloud open to continuous alteration. Some alterations will be cooperative, others not. It is possible that this fluidity could become more important to organisations than consistency, because IUIs can make empowerment, participation, and fluidity extremely important to a target audience as we shall see in the next chapters.

Messages, audiences, media. To recap: the appearance of IUIs affects three of PR's main components. Because of that, many PR activities must be changed. These changes will largely not be made by changes to the speed or volume of information; they will be based on engaging our individual imaginations and our participation in the PR process including its challenges to our conscience. Humans are already having trouble living in peace with social media and when specialists in human computer interaction write that 'the affective [emotion] system aims at human-system interaction and evoking emotions on purpose, while the goal of affect-aware software is to support certain processes' (Landowska et al., 2016, p. 740), we must reflect on what it means for our view of communication. The search for answers involves understanding the new connections we will have with organisations that will use IUIs to influence us.

These opening remarks hopefully offer enough reasons to treat IUIs as a distinct subject for PR to think about. Enough reasons too for us to ask, in the long-term, if a connection to IUIs could reach a point where PR continues functioning but looks like something else altogether.

References

Bernays, E. L. (2005). *Propaganda: With an introduction by Mark Crispin Miller.* New York: Ig.
Boyd, L. H., Boyd, W. L., & Vanderheiden, G. C. (1990). The graphical user interface: Crisis, danger, and opportunity. *Journal of Visual Impairment & Blindness, 84*(10), 496–502. Retrieved from https://files.eric.ed.gov/fulltext/ED333687.pdf.
Fogg, B. J. (2003). *Persuasive technology: Using computers to change what we think and do.* Amsterdam: Elsevier.
Fogg, B. J. (2008, June). Mass interpersonal persuasion: An early view of a new phenomenon. In H. Oinas-Kukkonen, M. Harjumaa, P. Hasle, P. Øhrstrøm, K. Segerståhl (Eds). *International conference on persuasive technology* (pp. 23–34). Berlin and Heidelberg: Springer.
Hildebrand, C., & Bergner, A. (2019). Detrimental trust in automation: How conversational robo advisors leverage trust and mis-calibrated risk taking.

ACR North America Advances in Consumer Research, 47, 123–128. Retrieved from https://www.acrwebsite.org/volumes/v47/acr_vol47_2552187.pdf.

Jaquero, V. L., Montero, F., Molina, J. P., & Gonz, P. (2009). Intelligent user interfaces: Past, present and future. In M. Redondo, C. Bravo, M. Ortega (Eds.), *Engineering the User Interface* (pp. 1–12), London: Springer.

Landowska, A., Szwoch, M., & Szwoch, W. (2016). Methodology of affective intervention design for intelligent systems. *Interacting with Computers, 28*(6), 737–759.

Lee, I. L. (1934). *The problem of international propaganda: A new technique necessary in developing understanding between nations.* Occasional Papers – No. 3. New York: Published privately.

Marx, K., Fowkes, B., & Mandel, E. (1990). *Capital: A critique of political economy.* London: Penguin.

McLuhan, M., & Gordon, W. T. (2011). *The Gutenberg galaxy: The making of typographic man.* eBook. Toronto: University of Toronto Press. First published 1966.

McLuhan, M., & Gordon, W. T. (2013). *Understanding media: The extensions of man.* E-book. New York: Gingko Press. First published 1964.

Microsoft Technology Licensing, LLC. (2019). US Patent application for visualization of training dialogs for a conversational bot. patent application (Application #20200334568). Retrieved from https://patents.justia.com/patent/20200334568.

Negroponte, N. (1996). *Being digital.* New York: Vintage Books.

PR Week. (2021). *Reshaping the future in an ever-changing present.* Webcast, March 9, 2021. Registration page. Retrieved from https://onlinexperiences.com/scripts/Server.nxp?LASCmd=AI:4;F:QS!10100&ShowUUID=C539FA33-CD3F-4E2E-B566-7B9E98B441E7&AffiliateData=030921-WEB

Shannon, C. E. (1948). A mathematical theory of communication. *The Bell System Technical Journal, 27*(3), 379–423. Retrieved from https://pure.mpg.de/rest/items/item_2383162_7/component/file_2456978/content

Shrager, J., & Finin, T. (1982, August). An expert system that volunteers advice. *Proceedings of the second annual national conference on artificial intelligence (AAAI-82).* Palo Alto, CA: AAAI.

Sonntag, D. (2017). Intelligent user interfaces: A tutorial. arXiv preprint arXiv:1702.05250. Retrieved from https://arxiv.org/ftp/arxiv/papers/1702/1702.05250.pdf

Xiao, R., Cao, T., Guo, N., Zhuo, J., Zhang, Y., & Harrison, C. (2018, April). LumiWatch: On-arm projected graphics and touch input. *Proceedings of the 2018 CHI conference on human factors in computing systems* (pp. 1–11). New York: Association for Computing Machinery. Retrieved from https://static1.squarespace.com/static/564b5107e4b087849452ea4b/t/5ae4ec85352f-53e6c782202d/1524952203900/LumiWatch.pdf

Xiao, R., Hudson, S., & Harrison, C. (2016, November). DIRECT: Making touch tracking on ordinary surfaces practical with hybrid depth-infrared sensing. *Proceedings of the 2016 ACM international conference on interactive surfaces and spaces* (pp. 85–94). New York: Association for Computing Machinery. Retrieved from https://static1.squarespace.com/static/564b5107e-4b087849452ea4b/t/591c69621b10e37f47ec2354/1495034217345/direct.pdf

Yin, X., Wang, H., Yin, P., & Zhu, H. (2019). Agent-based opinion formation modeling in social network: A perspective of social psychology. *Physica A: Statistical Mechanics and Its Applications, 532*(121786), 549–561.

2 Immersive communication
Virtual and augmented realities

Sight, touch, interfaces and PR: points of convergence

Jung worried that from the nineteenth century on 'scientific materialism' had created a 'psychology without the soul' where 'everything that could not be seen with the eyes or touched with the hands was held in doubt' (Jung, 1955, p. 173). Whether one agrees with this view or not, Jung touches on a human trait which predates scientific materialism but not strategic communication. Humans want to reinforce experience with the proofs of sight and touch: a parent looking into the eyes of a baby; the golden touch of Croesus; doubting Thomas reaching for Christ's wounds. Sight, touch, revelation, and belief are closely related, and often in that order. Science's faith in the material descends from an older faith. PR similarly originated in unscientific and premodern efforts to manage our senses and beliefs. Watching and touching IUIs are products of the 'scientific materialism' noted by Jung but they must understand and satisfy the same ancient instincts as PR.

Rules about watching or touching people or things have long been used as media and messages. People in organisations often try to be noticed or touched by someone senior to them, or feel stronger emotion when under their direct gaze. Fans mob a sporting hero after a big game; and camera crews think of ways to make us feel close to a celebrity. We touch and inspect interesting new possessions, interfaces included. Sight and touch are managed with especial care when power is to be communicated. They are controlled; rationed or permitted in particular ways, as in the managed appearances of star CEOs, heads of state, or athletes. In conveying an impression of power or glamour, sight can become as tactile as touch, in an almost magical transition. A journalist watched a crowd petitioning Emperor Haile Selassie of Ethiopia, King of Kings, Lion of Judah:

DOI: 10.4324/9781003111320-2

Let's say that the Imperial gaze just grazes your face – just grazes! You could say that it was really nothing, but on the other hand, how could it really be nothing, when it did graze you?

(Kapuściński, 1989, p. 14)

Seeing and touching can also be used to communicate misfortune, isolation, humiliation, or punishment, but PR usually exists to persuade or motivate, and manages sight and touch to obtain cooperative responses. IUIs are learning to do the same and for the same reason. They can converge and collaborate productively with PR, with their own versions of sight and touch.

Sight

Virtual worlds

By sight, we mean an IUI that may have sight of its own, or is able to track or augment our own sight. Curve, a project by Columbia University's Computer Graphics and User Interfaces (CGUI) Laboratory, allows users to visit an urban setting, either using VR or AR (Augmented Reality) while receiving and collecting data about it (Wu et al., 2013, p. 41). Instead of simply presenting data, Mise-Unseen is a system that tracks the user's gaze to unnoticeably modify the VR scene observed by the user. Besides these more covert actions, systems can also support users in detecting new angles for observing, and interesting objects outside their view or hidden by other objects (Sukan et al., 2014; Yu et al., 2019).

IUIs will take our eyes into a world that it can interpret for us, and which is far more sophisticated than the virtual worlds now available. Future worlds may be real, virtual, or a hybrid of real and virtual (i.e. augmented). Virtual and augmented spaces are going to be vivid and compelling, perhaps sophisticated and sovereign with their own rules and citizens, complex economic activity, philosophies, and forms of faith beyond, for instance, the possibilities in Altspace, an existing virtual world which has a VR Church (AltspaceVR 2021). A like-minded audience is likely to prefer a customised VR and AR society peopled with like-minded avatars, and where particular views, temptations, or tastes are reinforced and not challenged or chipped away, as they are every day in the exhausting business of living in the real world. The interfaces will be responsive to our passing or permanent preferences. They may in time, as we shall see later, be able to disconnect our minds from headsets or other purely external tools, and perhaps from our sensory organs that guide our touch, taste, sound, smell, and sight.

PR will enter those worlds. PR goes wherever emotions can be stimulated and messages designed. Is there any reason then, why organisations would not conduct PR with IUIs offering virtual and augmented realities? VR visitors may, for instance, want real world government services to be available in their virtual spaces. At a basic level this has already happened. In 2007, Sweden opened a virtual 'Embassy' in the Virtual World of Second Life, siting it on the Stockholm archipelago and opening it with a ribbon cutting ceremony (Government Technology, 2007). Second Life, launched in 2003, is currently the largest virtual world. Its currency is the Linden Dollar (worth US$0.00313 at July 21, 2021 exchange rates).

Other virtual worlds may be made for particular situations, perhaps as affordable alternatives to real-world alternatives. In 2014, an interface headset was used to immerse clinicians into a simulated hospital, modelled on a real London hospital that was coping with a local disaster (Pucher et al., 2014). Sony Innovation Studios in California works with Atom View, a volumetric video technology software made to capture 'quadrillions and quintillions of data points' from all angles, to place entertainers in virtual worlds essentially equivalent to a real world assembled from atoms (Cook et al., 2019); 'preserving matter one atom at a time,' in the words of the promotional video (Sony Innovation Studios, 2020).

What does this suggest about IUI, PR, and sight? A 1996 research paper considered the prospects for user interfaces and 'virtual environments' (VE), and noted some interesting distinctions, as far as PR is concerned:

> The term *immersion* is used to describe the mental state of users of a VE when they feel as though they are directly engaged with the objects in the virtual world. This might also be termed *cognitive immersion* to contrast it with *sensory immersion*, which typically involves providing synthetic stimuli to users' visual, auditory, tactile and kinaesthetic channels in order to increase cognitive immersion.
>
> (Hand, 1996, p. 1)

Some multisensory and wearable interfaces attempt to merge cognitive and sensory and provide what some researchers have called 'telepresence' or the sense of being immersed in an environment from a distance, integrating sensor technologies with the sensory system of whatever is being experienced or controlled; a robot, for instance. They are used in many settings including offices, education, rehabilitation, gaming and entertainment as well as training, military exercises, and space research (Martinez-Hernandez et al., 2017, p. 1). Much immersive research centres on external interfaces like headsets. Others wish to expand the human nervous system's role as an interface circuit. The Future Interfaces Group at Carnegie Mellon University has developed a wearable interface that lets us interact with a watch using the skin of the arm (FIG, 2019), thus extending the interactive space of the small screen of the watch. The same technology can also be used in VR, employing our forearm instead of gestures to act in the virtual world (Zhang et al., 2019).

The possibilities of an IUI based on our own circuitry, our own senses, and that can send the user into virtual and augmented realities, is presumably of interest to human agents of persuasion. Might travel and tourism companies engage with audiences and their influencers by virtually immersing them in the experience of a destination? Perhaps marching with legionaries on Hadrian's Wall, zip lining in Costa Rica, or enjoying afternoon tea at a luxury hotel in Istanbul? Might PR be able to offer a host of such experiences? Could PR immerse a quadriplegic person in its messages as equally and totally as any other audience? Or a housebound elderly person? Could homebuyers experience a property right down to its wiring, or activists create the outcomes of a preferred policy? Would we enter VR to experience the apology of an erring celebrity? How could such immersive PR help companies launch products? Could a company walk investors more persuasively through its latest restructuring?

Eye tracking

Other interfaces want to learn what we like to see in virtual and real environments, tracking our eye movements with sensors, algorithms, projectors, headsets; monitoring light reflections, targeting areas of gaze, looking for patterns; constantly creating, in the words of one tracking company 'the conditions for new insights into human behavior and intuitive user interfaces' (Tobii, 2020). Humans are growing more used to the idea of eye tracking. Software and devices by Mirametrix, GazePoint, Tobii, and others are used for eye tracking in VR and AR, on webcams, on PCs and laptops, or in mobile devices. Those trying to divine the truths told by eye movement include marketers, supermarket chains, the medical profession, caregivers of people with degenerative illnesses, the military, tech companies, safety and ergonomic experts in the workplace (Eberling, 2019), and the legal profession. In 2017, a person almost immobilised by Motor Neuron Disease used eye tracking to help convict his childhood abuser in a British court (Bowcott, 2017). Most famously, eye tracking helped Stephen Hawking enlarge our understanding of time and space.

Other, more ambiguous possibilities are also raised for PR's consideration. As eye-tracking technology becomes more affordable and its interfaces less invasive, organisations may believe they can 'investigate the cognitive processes underlying visual experience (e.g. attention, preference, discrimination)' (Gibaldi et al., 2017, p. 923). In other words, investigate our gaze for biases. Interfaces like those are building on widespread agreement that 'Gaze behavior reflects cognitive processes and can give hints of our thinking and intentions. We often look at things before acting on them' (Majaranta & Bulling, 2014, p. 39). Our eyes give away our secret preferences. Eye tracking can, it is argued, tell truths about the mind behind the choice. If this is true, eye tracking can reveal our enduring (or momentary) authentic beliefs and desires on particular subjects, and perhaps show PR how to engage them in a helpful way. Is any of this useful to PR practitioners dealing with a crisis, a societal issue, an organisation's identity, or an election campaign? It's been suggested that eye tracking is effective in measuring 'attentional bias' (perceiving certain things because of inbuilt bias towards them, while ignoring alternatives) thus 'supporting its use as a paradigm for studying selective attention to emotional stimuli in clinical and nonclinical populations' (Sears et al., 2019, p. 2759). Definitions of 'attentional bias', camouflaged by the apparently irrefutable and to many incomprehensible scientific objectivity of eye-tracking, may grow more self-serving or self-righteous outside a strictly clinical setting: how would that affect the strategic communication of governments, companies, and nonprofits?

There's no shortage of eye-tracking projects hinting at a future intersection with PR. A human-machine interfaces lab in Hungary and the National Bionics Programme are using electromyography (EMG – electrical activity to assess muscle health) to enhance a wearable eye tracker headset with gesture recognition, to help disabled people communicate and use electronic devices, and identify potentially dyslexic children (Ulbert Lab, 2020). The Human-automation Interaction and Cognition Lab (THInC) at the University of Michigan is interested in 'multimodal interfaces (including sight, sound, and touch) in support of human-computer interaction', and 'decision aids that support trust calibration' and understanding 'human error and error/disturbance management' (THInC Lab, 2020). Trust calibration (aligning expectations with outcomes) is particularly important in medical treatment. THInC is experimenting with desktop eye trackers to understand the impact of clutter on the ability of physicians to extract relevant patient information from Electronic Medical Records (Sarter, 2020). In September 2020, Facebook launched Project Aria, reported as a partnership with the makers of Ray-Ban to produce glasses that 'capture video, audio, eye-tracking and location data that Facebook can use to aid its development of augmented reality smart glasses'. Facebook workers wearing the glasses will be dressed in easily identifiable clothing, and identifiable details will be scrubbed from the captured images (Rodriguez, 2020).

Much of the language surrounding eye tracking may be described as vaguely objective or vaguely virtuous. Tracking usually seeks to 'understand', to 'aid, to 'support' the people being tracked. As with IUIs in general, such intentions can hardly be criticised, and the alternative meanings of the words are for the present left unexplored, understandably so when we think about the potential of eye tracking to help people with severe medical conditions, the housebound, air traffic controllers, shoppers trying to find what they want, or VR fans in search of a better Virtual World. The ease and near invisibility of some interfaces make human cooperation effortless. For a moment, there almost seems nothing for PR to discuss.

But if we are trying to 'understand' the individual being tracked, we must have a reason for doing it, stated or unstated. For time-pressed and competing organisations, understanding for its own sake has little value. It must contribute to an action. If communicators for a political party, campaign group, government, security agency, breakfast cereal, want to track eye movements including attentional bias, we may be doing it to help a business transaction, or to attract people to our ideas or products. PR will be doing it for these reasons, and to learn how to persuade us by aligning what it says and does with the tracked person's preferences. What might an intense desire to know us better mean for those of us who don't want our eyes to be tracked? Would it become as hard to avoid eye tracking as it is already hard to go through a day without being captured by security cameras? Could submitting to continuous observation become a pre-requisite for participating in civic society? What, for example, could political PR do with eye-tracking research seeking to understand why people pay less attention (fixation duration) to political posters from parties they don't support regardless of age, education, or gender (Marquart et al., 2016, p. 2587)? The research naturally suggested a next step: 'future research is strongly recommended to distinguish between exposure and avoidance effects'

(Marquart et al., 2016, p. 2588). How, in other words, can we make a political poster – or presumably any other political communication tool – more persuasive to more people? Would understanding eye tracking and attentional bias lead to actual policies being changed in response to voter concerns, or to better designed posters that present the existing message more persuasively? Are our opinions being sought, or are we being managed, or both?

PR, perpetually time-pressured, operating in highly complex societies, trying to squeeze complex information into the bite-size bits that most of us either prefer or can spare time for, will want to learn how to do it better by monitoring us on preferably inoffensive and unobtrusive interfaces. Will that include using eye tracking to 'understand' or 'help' us navigate detailed proposals? Or will it mean, as it often has in the past, designing virtual or real-world encounters with information presented in evermore compelling forms, to attract you or us to something we might not like if the same content was displayed differently or in more detail? Are we comfortable with the idea of eye tracking in politics or issues management, or should its use be limited?

Touch

In 1985 [writes Simon Moore], I shook the hand of one of Britain's first Trade Unionists. Joseph Arch was born in 1826 and died in 1919. Mister Arch's hands, small and delicate for a man who began work on the land when he was nine, were plaster casts. They are kept at the Museum of English Rural Life, at Reading University. The casts were made for reasons unknown, but taking casts of limbs and faces was common in the past and is not unknown today for occasions like birth or death.

Joseph Arch was well known in Victorian Britain. Like many other Victorian public figures, his personality could be conveyed in new ways to a population which was becoming more literate: his words could be reported by the press, his face captured in photographs and engravings. It also appears that at least someone wanted to come as close to touching him as the technology of the day permitted.

Touch is hard for media to communicate, to borrow a phrase, second hand. What if, though, a prosthetic offered the sensation of touch, and a more natural interface for the wearer? Telesurgery already uses a robot guided by a surgeon from far away. What if a surgeon can investigate or operate on a virtual body with the added benefits of touch? What if a person in mourning could feel the face of their loved one? A parent touch an infant in an incubator, or a partner in prison? What if we could touch the fabric of a dress we are thinking about purchasing online? What if, reverting to public relations, a politician, celebrity or activist – the Joseph Arches of our own time – could shake the hands or bump the fists of a million people simultaneously? Could that be a useful communication asset and in which circumstances? What if PR could create a virtual event – perhaps the launch of a video game – which offered touch as well as sight and sound? Some games already offer primitive tactile experiences using vibration. Could future games offer a far richer experience of touch? What if, moving to issues management, an anti-vivisection nonprofit invited social media influencers to feel the quivering body of an animal? Or a marine conservation group reproduced the laboured movements of a whale stranded on a beach?

Haptic technology simulates touch for the user. Virtual touch tries to offer sensations of reality whether that reality is virtual or real. A haptic interface brings the user in closer touch with those worlds, either on its own or working with other sense-arousing technologies. Haptics studies hands, feet, and skin as closely as eye tracking studies eyes. It investigates ways to stimulate the hand's receptors and nerves with 'mechanical, thermal, and chemical stimuli' (Durlach & Mavor, 1995). Research in virtual touch, when many people can feel the same thing at once, or when a single person feels something independently, takes a special interest in interface innovation, producing new information (and therefore communication) opportunities for PR's consideration. Some groups are experimenting with soft materials that are more responsive to touch. Stanford University's CHARM (Collaborative Haptics in Robotics and Medicine) Lab has investigated 'particle jamming' (Stanley & Okamura, 2015), using granulated material, in this case a 'digital clay' composed of coffee grounds, with a membrane – silicon rubber and air – to change the rigidity and shape of the interface to match a virtually desirable surface. 'Can we change the way that things feel' CHARM Lab's Principal Investigator asked an audience, 'so that when we reach out and touch them with as many fingers as you want, you experience something realistic?' (Okamura, 2013, 9:50).

Haptics research also seeks to achieve tactile *localisation*, or feeling a touch on a particular part of the body; and *discrimination*, knowing if we are being touched with a two point or one-point device. It is no small matter in medical training, and a reason why 'Emerging research in haptics aims to create soft material technologies for use in interfaces that can deliver programmable tactile feedback' (Reardon et al., 2020, p. 7). The RE Touch Lab at University of California, Santa

Barbara, imitates membranes, filaments, and sensors for the electronic capture of stresses to achieve an object's shape, for example, 'to image simulated tumours in phantom tissues' (Visell, 2018, 18:21), or to help restore a sense of touch in cases where nerves in hand or arm have been damaged but retain some connectivity.

Ultimately, haptics seeks to eliminate the differences between biological and simulated touch, to the point where a hand might as easily be a constructed prosthetic. 'We envision', wrote the designers of the soft interface just described, 'new applications of such soft tactile interfaces in many arenas, including soft interfaces for expressive multimedia performance, soft interfaces for tactile communication, and programmable soft control panels for automotive cockpits' (Reardon et al., 2020, p. 13). Included in that, perhaps, will be public relations managed moments which use touch in ways like the ones just described. Touch is too important for communicators to neglect and has not been neglected, as the long history of power relations and reputation management amply demonstrates. The replication and 'mass distribution' of simulated human-to-human, tactile engagement means haptic IUIs will play a part in PR, including sports and product PR, crisis and issues PR, healthcare PR, promotional events, entertainment, corporate PR, and community relations.

The haptic IUIs described here are not always attached to mobile technology. Many need us to go to them, and initiate the contact. Will there be a communication connection between haptics, robots and mobility? From the controlling side, in the words of one science journalist: 'Haptic guidance may become the preferred method to control robots in the future because it's more intuitive than sending written computer commands' (Amirtha, 2015). What are the PR possibilities of robotic IUIs with haptic interfaces who can come to us, whether we want them to or not? Mobile or not, could haptic interfaces capture our touch and communicate the experience to other IUIs and other human audiences? Could the nature of the touch be used by us or on us? Maybe to help assess enthusiasm for a client, or the strength of our attachment to a product, policy, identity or service? Or with a government, whether democratic, semi-democratic or wholly undemocratic? What are the implications for relations between IUI and human, when a haptic-capable IUI initiates the contact, not us? Could a totalitarian regime or ideology use haptic technology to become instantly acquainted with the inner feelings of citizens? What other questions does it raise for the organisation seeking our touch? The simulated hands of Joseph Arch's successors may be designed to respond to our touch submissively, warmly, coldly, indifferently, or dominantly, depending on the message that must be sent. Would this make the message more truthful or only more persuasive?

Such questions might matter less in some fields. It's hard to disagree with the principle of surgeon robots or robots assembling precision devices, or rescuing earthquake victims, or any other activity in which an interface's touch and sight could be lifesaving. Or good for the environment. At the European Space Agency, the Telerobotics and Haptics Laboratory has experimented with (human operated) robots equipped with haptic interfaces to retrieve space junk, including a 'fully haptic exoskeleton', 'cybergrasp glove', or 'Generic Hand Grasp Master' to manipulate virtual computer-generated objects with force-feedback (European Space Agency, 2020). Does it matter if such robots are human operated or fully autonomous? There is a continuum of control possibilities, from full control to completely delegated autonomy. Is human agency in haptics or in other interfaces even an issue in strategic communication as long as the cause is good? PR must start thinking about haptics, in part because the moral and operational impact of haptic interfaces will be shaped by what PR does with them. PR can move fast once convinced of a medium's value. As a public communication medium, the haptic interface may be adopted too quickly and widely for law and social conventions to keep up. The first responses to its powers and possibilities will be prompted by our individual senses, not by understandably cautious and slower-moving institutions, and the impact on us as individuals will be more profound than any laws or codes of conduct that develop from those first contacts.

Sight, touch, and the balance of communication

Strategic communication will learn to use IUIs creatively, extensively, overpoweringly, and with a superb sense of timing. That much is strongly suggested by PR's history with other media. Perhaps the main question raised by PR's use of virtual worlds and other watching and touching interfaces is about the communication power balance: between individual and organisation, leader and led, machine and human, senses and reason, and the organic and the inorganic. In our still-dominant non-virtual world, we have the chance to reflect on what is going to happen. As communicators for and with organisations we should recognise the persuasive potency of these interfaces, and use them to entertain and instruct. Sometimes – hopefully mitigated by prudence and wisdom – we will allow ourselves to be persuaded by them but not without the power to answer them back on at least equal communication terms. At the very least we must be able to change watching and touching interfaces as much as they will change us.

References

AltspaceVR. (2021). VR Church. Retrieved from https://account.altvr.com/worlds/1016889515295375453

Amirtha, T. (2015, September 16). Half man, half machine: The clever haptics-based system helping astronauts in space pilot robots on earth. ZDNet. Retrieved from https://www.zdnet.com/article/half-man-half-machine-the-clever-haptics-based-system-helping-astronauts-in-space-pilot-robots-on/

Bowcott, O. (2017, February 13). Dying man gives evidence with his eyes to help convict vicar who abused him. *The Guardian*. Retrieved from https://www.theguardian.com/uk-news/2017/feb/13/stephen-hawking-style-eye-tracking-tech-helped-convict-vicar-cyril-rowe-of-child-abuse

Cook, A. V., Berman, J., & Dajee, J. (2019, January 16). Intelligent interfaces. *Deloitte Insights*. Retrieved from https://www2.deloitte.com/us/en/insights/focus/tech-trends/2019/human-interaction-technology-intelligent-interface.html

Durlach, N. I., & Mavor, A. S. (1995). *Virtual reality: Scientific and technological challenges*. Washington, DC: National Academies Press.

Eberling, J. (2019). When eye-tracking is used as an interface. *LEAD Innovation Management Blog*. Retrieved from https://www.lead-innovation.com/english-blog/eye-tracking-as-an-interface

European Space Agency. (2020). Enabling & support. *Telerobotics and Haptics Laboratory*. Retrieved from http://www.esa.int/Enabling_Support/Space_Engineering_Technology/Telerobotics_Haptics_Laboratory

FIG. (2019). *Actitouch*. Future Interfaces Group, Carnegie Mellon University. Retrieved from http://www.figlab.com/#/actitouch-2019/

Gibaldi, A., Vanegas, M., Bex, P. J., & Maiello, G. (2017). Evaluation of the Tobii EyeX Eye tracking controller and Matlab toolkit for research. *Behavior Research Methods, 49*(3), 923–946. Retrieved from https://link.springer.com/article/10.3758/s13428-016-0762-9

Government Technology. (2007, May 31). Sweden inaugurates virtual embassy. Retrieved from https://www.govtech.com/e-government/Sweden-Inaugurates-Virtual-Embassy.html

Hand, C. (1996, May). Some user interface issues for hypermedia virtual environments. In *5th International World-Wide Web Conference*. Retrieved from https://www.researchgate.net/profile/Chris_Hand3/publication/239065032_Some_User_Interface_Issues_for_Hypermedia_Virtual_Environments/links/55ab6df408ae481aa7fbd99e/Some-User-Interface-Issues-for-Hypermedia-Virtual-Environments.pdf

Jung, C. G. (1955). *Modern man in search of a soul*. eBook. New York City: Harcourt Brace.

Kapuściński, R. (1989). *The Emperor: Downfall of an autocrat.* New York: Vintage.

Majaranta, P., & Bulling, A. (2014). Eye tracking and eye-based human–computer interaction. In S. Fairclough, (Ed). *Advances in physiological computing* (pp. 39–65), London: Springer. Retrieved from https://www.perceptualui.org/publications/majaranta14_apc.pdf

Marquart, F., Matthes, J., & Rapp, E. (2016). Selective exposure in the context of political advertising: A behavioral approach using eye-tracking methodology. *International Journal of Communication, 10,* 20. Retrieved from https://ijoc.org/index.php/ijoc/article/viewFile/4415/1667

Martinez-Hernandez, U., Boorman, L. W., & Prescott, T. J. (2017). Multisensory wearable interface for immersion and telepresence in robotics. *IEEE Sensors Journal, 17*(8), 2534–2541.

Okamura, A. (2013, June 20). Touch, engineered: Allison Okamura at TEDxStanford. TEDX Talks. Retrieved from https://www.youtube.com/watch?v=pPKqW3tdWCQ

Pucher, P. H., Batrick, N., Taylor, D., Chaudery, M., Cohen, D., & Darzi, A. (2014). Virtual-world hospital simulation for real-world disaster response: Design and validation of a virtual reality simulator for mass casualty incident management. *Journal of Trauma and Acute Care Surgery, 77*(2), 315–321.

Reardon, G., Kastor, N., Shao, Y., & Visell, Y. (2020, March). Elastowave: Localized tactile feedback in a soft haptic interface via focused elastic waves. In *2020 IEEE Haptics Symposium (HAPTICS)* (pp. 7–14). IEEE. Retrieved from https://rtlab.s3.amazonaws.com/reardon2020elastowave.pdf

Rodriguez, S. (2020, September 16). Facebook teaming up with Ray-Ban maker for first smart glasses in 2021. *CNBC.* Retrieved from https://www.cnbc.com/2020/09/16/zuckerberg-facebook-to-release-its-first-pair-of-smart-glasses-with-luxottica-.html

Sarter, N. (2020). *THinC Lab – Nadine Sarter.* Center for Ergonomics, University of Michigan. Retrieved from https://c4e.engin.umich.edu/research/ergonomics-laboratories/thinc-lab-professor-nadine-sarter/

Sears, C., Quigley, L., Fernandez, A., Newman, K., & Dobson, K. (2019). The reliability of attentional biases for emotional images measured using a free-viewing eye-tracking paradigm. *Behavior Research Methods, 51*(6), 2748–2760.

Sony Innovation Studios. (2020). *Atom View video.* 2:17. United States: Sony. Retrieved from December 12, 2020 https://sites.sonypictures.com/sonyinnovationstudios/site/

Stanley, A. A., & Okamura, A. M. (2015). Controllable surface haptics via particle jamming and pneumatics. *IEEE Transactions on Haptics, 8*(1), 20–30.

Sukan, M., Elvezio, C., Oda, O., Feiner, S., & Tversky, B. (2014, October). ParaFrustum: Visualization techniques for guiding a user to a constrained set of viewing positions and orientations. *Proceedings of the 27th annual ACM symposium on user interface software and technology,* (pp. 331–340). New York: Association for Computing Machinery.

THinC Lab. (2020). *Homepage welcome.* THinC Lab, University of Michigan. Retrieved from https://thinclab.engin.umich.edu/

Tobii. (2020). About. Tobii Group. Retrieved from https://www.tobii.com/group/about/

Ulbert Lab. (2020). Eye-tracking and gesture recognition. Retrieved from http://www.ulbertlab.com/human-machine-interface-lab

Visell, Y. (2018, July 9). Haptics: Science and engineering for the sense of touch. *University of California Television.* Retrieved from https://www.youtube.com/watch?v=bdgmGrESe14

Wu, H. K., Lee, S. W. Y., Chang, H. Y., & Liang, J. C. (2013). Current status, opportunities and challenges of augmented reality in education. *Computers & Education, 62,* 41–49.

Yu, D., Liang, H. N., Fan, K., Zhang, H., Fleming, C., & Papangelis, K. (2019). Design and evaluation of visualization techniques of off-screen and occluded targets in virtual reality environments. *IEEE Transactions on Visualization and Computer Graphics.* Piscataway: IEEE. Retrieved from https://difeng.me/papers/19_Wedge.pdf

Zhang, Y., Kienzle, W., Ma, Y., Ng, S. S., Benko, H., & Harrison, C. (2019, October). ActiTouch: Robust touch detection for on-skin AR/VR interfaces. *Proceedings of the 32nd annual ACM symposium on user interface software and technology,* (pp. 1151–1159). New York: Association for Computing Machinery. Retrieved from https://yangzhang.dev/research/ActiTouch/ActiTouch.pdf

3 Artificial intelligence, emotions, and trust

Feeling is believing

IUIs and feelings

Ideally, a PR-friendly IUI should read emotion, respond to emotion, perhaps show emotion, and continually learn from interactions with human emotion. We're still assuming (as we are throughout this book) that at least some interfaces will need to persuade humans to take a course of action, or listen to humans and accommodate their views. This chapter thinks about IUIs with emotion capabilities ('emotional IUIs' for short), their need to build trust with human users, and PR's future with technologies using emotion and trust to 'account for the unique circumstances of the user' (Morris et al., 2018, p. 1).

Humans use emotion to interpret data and guide decisions. Emotion (or 'affect') is a short-cut to action and frequently overrides the more time-consuming task of synthesising information in volume. Emotion affects our views of organisations, individuals, ideas, beliefs, and products. Emotion can help us form close connections with inanimate, inorganic, and wholly immaterial objects. Emotion's connection to motivation 'explains the direction and magnitude of behavior' (Gooch et al., 2016, p. 6). PR must rouse or direct that emotion, and IUIs that interpret or express emotion in the right way at the right time may help PR reach its target audiences.

IUIs are learning about emotions, for the same reasons:

> In order to increase the effectiveness and acceptance of a new generation of Human Computer Interfaces (HCI) these interfaces would need to show human-like behavior and be sensitive and responsive to emotions of their communication partner. This sensitivity and expressivity is of importance in human interaction and actually transmits a lot of valuable information.
>
> (van der Heide & Trivino, 2010, p. 1)

DOI: 10.4324/9781003111320-3

At present, some IUIs are trying to mimic and read emotion in voices, in graphic displays that also read emotion in texts (using sentiment analysis and natural language processing) and facial expressions, and to a limited extent in robots. The general idea is that the better the interface accommodates humans, the better it understands humans, the more humans will trust it, and – thanks to an IUI's emotional capabilities – cement that trust with their feelings. The prospects for humans accepting and even welcoming machine mastery of emotion are good. The point has already been made that more and more of our private world, including our personal communication traits, is being exposed for public scrutiny, because as a species we cannot resist extending our 'self' into any platform that helps us engage with others and harvest information, including information about other people's feelings. IUIs are another step on this journey, which could join organisations with people more closely. Emotional IUIs might be able to breach the walls separating external experience from inner selfhood. In that connection and in parenthesis, maybe the ultimate shared objective for PR and IUIs is to take organisations deeper into what Jung called our Unconscious self. Jung himself did not welcome this possibility. Towards the end of his life, he repeatedly warned that the Unconscious self was under threat from ideas and organisations, and their ideological and commercial subversion of once-spiritual symbols that nourished our Unconscious.

What could 'machined emotion' do for PR, people, and organisations? PR's objectives are frequently qualitative: emotional IUIs must be able to crystallise feeling around a vague idea or identity, or something as multifaceted, changeable, and hard to pin down as a reputation. Intelligent interfaces working in other fields, seeking a straight exchange of data for services like collecting financial information or dispatching shipments, might not have to be as emotionally advanced in what would be comparatively straightforward encounters with human users.

Having said that, most IUIs might benefit from some emotional intelligence, whatever their function. What has been said of voice user interfaces can be said about other kinds of IUIs: 'when a person speaks to or listens to a voice user interface, the person assumes a certain amount of emotional involvement with the interface' (Clayton & Jones, 2008). Reciprocating that involvement would help an IUI respond appropriately to users. An interchange could be compromised or ended if the user is emotionally dissatisfied with the encounter. They could go elsewhere to find emotional responses to help them want to complete a transaction, weigh evidence, and form a perception. A preferred interface might even be quite primitive and yet be capable of building an emotional connection with the user.

One way to achieve emotional involvement, it is proposed, is for IUIs to communicate as 'naturally' as possible, showing a user that there is emotional sympathy inside the device. There is as yet no reason for us to think such sympathy is 'genuine', beyond an irrational instinct thrown up by our fast-moving and changing feelings. But, of course, irrationality – maybe a less loaded expression is 'non-rationality' – doesn't make imaginative assumptions of sympathy less useful for interfaces or PR practitioners. A 'non-rational' connection between human and machine would only be helped by an interface that reduced emotion to its constituent molecules, and knew when and how to re-configure those parts to suit a situation. Affective (emotion-aware) computing is an attempt to construct ontologies (which in this case refers to the essential elements and connections) of 'affective' states, to get better reads of facial expressions and voice modulation. Some interface designers are adapting their public image to reflect the new possibilities. MIT's affective computing work leverages emotion AI as an additional communication. It 'combines engineering and computer science with psychology, cognitive science, neuroscience, sociology, education, psychophysiology, value-centered design, ethics, and more' (MIT, 2020). PR practitioners should be able to clearly see communi-cation potential in the group's stated goal 'of bringing together Emo-tion AI [artificial intelligence] and other affective technologies in order to make people's lives better' (MIT, 2021, Overview).

Meanwhile, another research team hopes that affective computing will:

> complete the development of intelligent systems by enabling them to automatically interact with users and to make their own deci-sions when emitting responses, without any human intervention. Thus, the common goals of users and intelligent systems can be achieved more effectively.
> (Garay-Vitoria et al., 2019, p. 40503)

At the very least, affective IUIs should let PR use its human capital more effectively, maybe by needing fewer humans to put a 'human' face on the client. MIT's interface projects show how this might hap-pen by designing technology which offers a more personal connection to information:

> Using state of the art small, wearable sensors and powerful ma-chine learning technologies we have an opportunity to design

radically different, highly personalized solutions for assistive communication.

(MIT, 2021, Projects)

Psychophysiological computing, a part of affective computing, wants to understand the reasons for our feelings and how organic or artificial nervous systems can capture, change, or express them. Emotional AI is the technology used to carry those systems. Interfaces stimulating or expressing empathy on behalf of AI are already being designed for certain situations; for instance, to help improve communication and collaboration in cases of dyslexia and autism (Wang et al., 2019; Zhang et al., 2019). MIT's Commalla project wants to *capture* feeling and is being designed to assist minimally verbal individuals, including people with Autistic Spectrum Disorders or Down Syndrome. By capturing particular vocalisations, the project aims to understand and interpret the 'emotions, needs, and social exchanges' of the vocaliser, with small, wearable, recorders to collect the vocalisations and smart apps for caregivers to classify data remotely without any in-person interaction.

The automotive industry is particularly interested in affective interfaces that *change* feelings. One project involving several academic institutions and BMW's New Technologies research group wants to influence as well as read the emotions of drivers:

> Affective automotive user interfaces show potential for an improvement of driver safety through the detection of performance-influencing states, such as anger, and their mitigation through strategic interaction.

(Braun et al., 2019, p. 1)

The group's work points towards 'natural' interfaces that nudge rather than command, where the interface's message is helped by light effects and tone of voice, and – at least in the development stage – by eye tracking and measuring emotional arousal of the skin:

> We suggest natural voice interaction with subliminal cues (e.g., light) as suitable modalities for an interaction with positive outcome and recommend a strategic focus on empathy, without patronizing the user.

(Braun et al., 2019, p. 2)

Emotion detection and recognition is already a growing field, and we've just seen that 'emotional IUIs' is a perhaps slightly overcooked phrase for IUIs that can read human emotion. What are the prospects for the next step: IUIs that can *express* emotion beyond reading and trying to influence our emotions; that can respond with their own emotions, beyond that uncanny even-temperedness and visual design that many interfaces already seem to possess, and which can sometimes feel standardised? Some of the early 'emotional interfaces' were the chatbots whose avatars tended to be women with long, flowing hair. And then later, the equivalent on the men's side.

Potential advantages of emotionally expressive IUIs include, as one interface designer suggests, the chance 'to use humans' ability to act on emotions to create better user engagement' (Kuznetsov, 2019). Displays of emotion would be connected to a device's ability to read emotion in others, and to learn from its encounters. Emotional expressiveness might be included in enhanced graphic displays, in avatars, in virtual or augmented reality, in written and spoken words, and perhaps, in the case of haptics, with touch. At present, showing emotions properly seems harder for IUIs than reading emotions. Harder, but maybe not impossible. 'There is nothing magical about human emotions' an AI future watcher observed in 2019 (Rochon, 2019). After all, we can already create animations that make people connect, laugh, or cry. For interfaces supporting the elderly to age in place (Mynatt et al., 2000), or helping children with learning challenges, the advantages of emotional IUIs look very clear. For interfaces serving in combat or policing roles, the long-term consequences may be more debatable, possibly depending on whose side they are on; perhaps as debatable as an emotional interface coaxing us to believe something about a policy, brand, ideology, or government; encouraging us to reciprocate with feeling, and then measuring, recording, and recalibrating a response. This might help both sides know each other better but it might also ensure a lopsided PR relationship in which the interface media has superior communication skills than its human target audiences, especially when coupled with enforcement power.

It is sometimes said that 'humans' can control relations with a device by deciding what emotions the device can express through its interface. Certain humans might be able to do this to start with, but not humans in general. The reassurance of human ownership of interfaces is as problematic in its own way as machine control. Ultimate human control may be dressed up as 'collective', 'communal', 'people's', 'democratic', or 'human' but such terms risk being meaningless in an IUI context. Will all human IUI designers have the same noble or base motives, principles, ideals, objectives? Or the people paying them: all politicians, all PR practitioners, activist groups, brand managers, governments? Will everyone follow the same rules and interpret them in the same way? And if IUIs are equipped with Machine Learning, could an artificial agent (AA) adapt a programmed emotion beyond the boundaries set by its designer? and Are the limits of these machine-learned boundaries unknown? Science fiction regularly explores the possibilities of tech overreach. Should 'science fact' pay closer attention to interface overreach? Some reflection on this is necessary from a PR perspective. In 2006, Walmart's recommender system took people looking for Planet of the Apes to movies about Martin Luther King Jr. The system's emergent behaviour (emergent behaviour is behaviour that is not deliberately programmed into the device) was affected by human cataloguing errors, and resulted in something that is highly offensive to society (NBC, 2006; Sinha, 2006). Moreover, could an emotionally evolving IUI in time become, for PR, a key public with an influence and autonomy of its own? Two maybe unexpected guides to this problem are the banking and insurance industries, who are interested in emotive interfaces that 're-humanise' relations between company and customer, in the words of a 2015 post by Accenture Insurance (Accenture Insurance Financial Services, 2015). Accenture's 2015 *Fjord Trends* report includes recommendations for emotive interfaces. They point to a role for strategic communicators:

* Find your brand's personality, and incorporate it into your digital touchpoints, i.e. infuse digital 'smiles' and infuse them into their ecosystems
* Think about emotionally responsive UI
* Use Emojis. Businesses should consider thinking about how to incorporate this language into their messaging, notification, and authentication platforms
* Start a robot strategy. How would your brand find a presence with retail robots soon acting as your digital delivery platform?

(Accenture, 2014, Slide 29)

Could an emotional IUI read and react to a user under stress and fine-tune its own emotion better or as well as a human doing the same job, who might feel reciprocal pressure and respond inappropriately? Would such a device be valuable to PR in crisis communication, political PR, community relations, soft power communication or employee engagement? Again, we face a version of the question asked throughout this book: how likely is it that insurance-industry IUIs with emotional abilities will interest other organisations with other objectives?

Other possibilities of interest to PR include brain-computer interfaces (BCIs), robots, and avatars. BCIs 'have the advantage of having access to the source of emotional processing, the brain' (Garcia-Molina et al., 2013, p. 17). The robotics industry is also interested in emotion as part of its quest for 'emotionally and socially believable robot and ICT interfaces' (Esposito et al., 2014, p. 624). Would it matter to PR if such interfaces can't express emotion exactly the same way as us? Not if we feel that an AI's available range of emotion does the job adequately, or in an appealing way. It may be better to be emotional but not human-like emotional. Emotional IUIs may have to show their feelings more obviously than humans, by exaggerated voice or expressions (Mäkäräinen et al., 2014). Researchers have studied the positive impact on humans of 'advanced' (exaggerated) smiles by avatars in a real-time conversation. One study reported that 'enhancing the smile on one's avatar can lead to more positive outcomes compared to when the smile is accurately mapped on the avatar' (Oh et al., 2016, p. 14). As we explore more fully in Chapter 4, we are entering the realm of the 'uncanny valley' which tries to understand when and how we will be ready to accept the humanlike qualities of advanced technologies like interfaces.

Eventually, BCIs may integrate so closely with the human nervous system that devices won't need external emotional expressions. Some of the possibilities for this form of perception-shaping were explored in a 2020 article for the Rand Corporation, 'Brain-Computer Interfaces are coming. Will we be ready?'

> Advanced BCI technology could be used to reduce pain or even regulate emotions. What happens when military personnel are sent into battle with a reduced sense of fear? And when they return home, what psychological side effects might veterans experience without their "superhuman" traits?
>
> (Norris, 2020)

We will shortly describe how BCIs are being developed for healthcare: in prosthetics, therapies, and in other assistive technologies, and we must not think PR should ignore the questions and opportunities they present. Emotions shape perception; perception affects choices; choices decide our actions and entrench attitudes. Competitive PR involves opening and closing minds: opening them to the messages of the organisation it represents, and closing them to competing messages. If that, and persuasion and relationship building are basic PR tasks, it is possible that all of us will experience considerable side effects from what PR will do with emotional interfaces in every field from warfare to healthcare.

IUIs and trust: can trust be designed?

Users must trust the interface and the artificial agent it represents, and trust is a feeling. Trust can be designed into interfaces as it is into other products, organisations, and people. We already interact with interfaces that simulate human feeling by voice or simple images, like the Emojis mentioned just now. We know IUI research is exploring developing interfaces that read and respond to human feeling more deeply, with the longer-term goal of IUIs that feel for themselves. Since PR must align feeling with an organisation's objectives, the need for trust becomes critical. Trust mitigates risk and an interface with emotion must be trusted by the user if the two are to connect productively. Trust emerges when, in the words of one early researcher:

> The user freely communicates her emotional state, that is, when it is in her best interests to do so, and when she feels that the information is secure and she has something to gain from it.
>
> (Hayes-Roth et al., 1998, p. 93)

PR's interest in trust is long-standing. 'There is no question' said a lengthy review of trust research written for the UK's Institute for Public Relations, 'that trust is a commodity that all organisations need in order to function more effectively and efficiently. Without trust, organisations are bogged down by suspicion, anger, cynicism and disappointment' (Rawlins, 2007, p. 8). PR multinational Edelman produces an annual trust barometer for governments and non-government organisations, based on surveys in every inhabited continent. Another review asserted 'trust, legitimacy and reflection' as crucial concepts for PR's future identity (Ihlen & Verhoeven, 2012, p. 170).

PR must work with the connection between emotion and trust. It assumes emotion is abundant and can be aroused, and (for a while) managed once it is aroused, and that trust is a rarer and more fragile phenomenon. To reach their potential as PR platforms, emotional IUIs should be trusted as well, so that the user is encouraged to express feelings and opinion. Trust is also needed to anthropomorphise organisations in helpful ways, which will involve endowing IUIs with trustable emotions. Trust is akin to faith, but perhaps less single-minded or absolute. Its variables as applied to PR include who or what is seeking our trust, and why. We might add to those our memories, histories, instincts, principles, and personal experiences. These affect trust, and the success of PR's persuasiveness, cooperativeness, and openness. PR may not be able to guarantee trust, but can IUI design encourage more trust, and perhaps strengthen it by learning more about us by monitoring our responses to the interface? Would a trustable interface have to be as human as possible? Research into Autonomous Vehicles (AVs) found that:

> Anthropomorphizing AVs by providing it a voice and simulating intelligent conversation did not merely achieve higher trust ratings, but also higher ratings of likability and intelligence.
>
> (Ruijten et al., 2018, p. 12)

Simulated voices may not be successful all the time and for every scenario. They may sometimes sound rather alienating. It's generally held, though, that human-to-machine interactions are reinforced when the human experiences trust, and folds that trust into the emotions evoked by the encounter, and into the information that both sides present or exchange. One challenge to trust between IUIs and human emotion is the problem mentioned earlier: PR's goals aren't always transaction-centred (buy this product, tell me your symptoms). PR's goals are often purely perception-centred (accept this version of our identity; sympathise with our beliefs, policies or actions on issues or crises, let us build a strong, long-term relationship with you). Strategic communication often has no objective beyond encouraging a general atmosphere of trust and likeability, so it will be easier to communicate about specific matters if and when they come up.

Could IUIs help PR lay firmer foundations for trust? It could depend on whether the IUI is owned by the organisation. Such IUI devices may act in roughly the same way as a website; a place where identity can be exclusively managed, free from third party 'adulteration'. Wholly owned IUIs could increase the places where users can meet an organisation on its own terms and discover its emotional identity, not on the terms of independent media professionals with preferences and needs of their own. Popular and wholly owned IUIs might allow an organisation's PR team to fully coordinate its trust-building and emotion-shaping capabilities. Another advantage may be that such an IUI could work with many people simultaneously and a particularly 'adaptive interface' would learn to adjust to each individual's unique preferences. Such trust-abled IUIs could become the most potent communication technology in history: building trust on an enormous scale by communing with once unreachable aspects of each user's individuality, instead of imperfectly broad appeals to a collective sentiment. If this is so the consequences will be profound for the public sphere.

Like research on interfaces and emotion, research on trust and interfaces often focuses on designing a system that works predictably for the user. For certain exchanges, there seems no reason to doubt the value to trust of a smoothly operating and satisfying process: what has been called the 'correlation between a user's reliance on a system and their trust level' (Yu et al., 2017, p. 316). The expectations of the user should be met. The interface should be understandable and predictable; in other words, intuitive. Thus, the IUI needs to be designed with the user in mind using human-centred design methods as should all interfaces, intelligent or not. No matter how intelligent and emotional an IUI, it must be designed for the user.

In those circumstances can trust be wholly achieved by good IUI design, which eventually would let PR manage trust by influencing our mental models with simulated but familiar emotions? If good design underpins today's simple transactions between IUIs and user, will it be true for PR's persuasion and relationship management activities?

Perhaps, but designing trust faces the same basic challenge of interface design in general, namely human complexity. 'The design of services that satisfy spontaneous needs to generate emotions in others requires the integration of numerous components' (Norman & Ortony, 2003, p. 12). PR needs to discover those components, and how interfaces use them. Trusted interfaces must be emotional interfaces and PR has no use for untrusted media, as long as the target audiences can choose between competing interfaces. The same complex human factors behind our attraction to interfaces influence our trust in them as media: they involve cognition, a sense of communing with technology as naturally we do with humans, a social context, and our perception of motives (see Atkinson & Clark, 2013). So far, the interfaces haven't grasped the full extent of human complexity. Perhaps for that reason we aren't ready to put our entire trust in artificial intelligence:

> As intelligent algorithms and autonomous systems become increasingly widespread, an important question arises as to whether we can trust such technology, especially when they are making decisions in critical situations.
>
> (Hastie et al., 2017, p. 261)

More trust would make the user more likely to let the interface to make critical decisions. The need for good trust design is recognised for technologies operating in 'high impact, time- and mission-critical functions' in health, defence, transportation, and industry (Atkinson & Clark, 2013, p. 1).

Interfaces have taken different approaches to the problem of unlocking trust, all of which may have something to be said for them. Much of the research involves practicalities of user experience. It may, for instance, be mutually important for IUIs and PR that trust connects with 'emotional branding' as measured by service performance, an assessment which joins feeling to function (Priya et al., 2017). A study of e-health in rural areas decided 'UI usability factors are essential elements in conveying the trustworthiness of a web-based system and do affect consumers' perception of trust in personal relationship-based information exchanges' (Fruhling & Lee, 2006, p. 305). E-Banking research also explores interface trust as a contributor to e-banking satisfaction (Bacinello et al., 2017). Attention has been paid to 'mega portal services' seen as the main drivers of trust and which may include some or all of the following 'Cs': Commerce, Communication, Customisation, Community, Content, Context, and Coordination (see, for instance, Rayport & Jaworski, 2001; Kim & Arnett, 2012).

Other more hands-on ways to mix user design and sensory stimulation may be attractive to PR practitioners. They include creating a sense of 'gamification', and perhaps the actual use of games in reputation management systems that build trust (Keser, 2003). Colours have also been related to trust in interface design. Research in 2016 called for more study of 'the effects of color priming, specifically its effects on the activation of the insular cortex' (Hawlitschek et al., 2016). Other assets are a trustworthy voice and conversation abilities, which we saw being used in vehicle interfaces to make us better drivers (Ruijten et al., 2018). Research on human-like software agents has explored trust as convenient 'mental shortcuts' to an action. It found 'humans do in fact reliably and consistently apply properties of trust used in assessing humans to anthropomorphic agent designs' (Green, 2010, p. xviii). Trust-building properties included optimum distance between eyes on the face, the proportions of the chin, length of steady eye contact, and achieving a normal human appearance (Green, 2010).

A 2019 study of Blockchain and trust took a similar approach to 'trust-building properties', but by emphasising the need for a design that communicated:

> honesty ensured by decentralisation and public ledger's transparency; expertise supported by miners' competence and hard

labour; predictability supported by the cryptographic protocol; and reputation supported by large companies' interest in Bitcoin. Findings also identified Blockchain's characteristics supporting the other dimensions of trust: ease of use grounded in ease and quick transactions; and limited risk due to transactions' low cost and the decentralised, unregulated nature of Blockchain which limits the risk of institutional power abuse.

(Khairuddin, 2019, p. 114)

Trust-building may or may not wholly define PR, but it is a major reason why PR will be interested in IUIs. IUI research supports PR's view that trust can be used 'to reduce complexity' (Valentini & Kruckeberg, 2011, p. 98). We've seen that IUI is exploring useful connections between trust and efficient design: the best background colours on an interface, the layout, navigation, graphics, text, aesthetics, simplicity, and ease of use (for instance, Frison et al., 2019; Hawlitschek et al., 2016; Hussein et al., 2020). Other experiments in human-computer interactions link trust to user personality, and try to identify which personality traits are most open to IUI-mediated trust. In the context of AI and trust, the concept of 'explainability' has also gained importance. An intelligent system needs to be able to explain its decisions. Better understanding of trust's relationship to 'personality' would help designers build feedback loops that in turn help machines predict human trust levels and persuasively explain decisions (Fahr & Irlenbusch, 2008; Zhou & Lu, 2011; Zhou et al., 2020). Trust feedback loops would work closely with emotional IUIs to better engage with our personality, revealed by monitoring our feelings and actions as we use the interface.

Like PR, IUIs are interested in combining emotion and trust to communicate more effectively. Like PR, IUIs want to know the foundations of perception. Like a PR practitioner, an IUI represents an organisation and needs an audience. A shared interest in emotion and trust gives PR and IUIs a shared interest in the people they must reach.

Feelings and trust: beyond humans, beyond PR?

This chapter has suggested that the consequences of cooperation between PR and emotional IUIs will be significant for society and the individual. The implications for PR go beyond deploying IUIs that read emotion, or which can express humanlike emotions, and treating them like any other media platform. Could IUIs, for instance, take over from human-run PR and build an 'emotional identity' for an entire organisation or a product, communicate it with brain-computer interfaces and adjust it to the emotional response of a human user? The official 'mood' of an organisation already changes with circumstances, and the changes can be communicated, if somewhat clumsily. If the personality of an organisation is contained in its internal structure and culture, its architecture, social media activity, product and supply chain, could it be contained much more dynamically in interfaces sensitive to the mood of diverse identities? Campaign groups can skilfully harness the emotional appeal of their causes. Would they be ready to push the boundaries of emotionally equipped IUIs, as many of them have tested the emotional limits of other kinds of media? Would a trusted financial interface use emotion to support an investment recommendation? Would a government interested in, say, overcoming a widespread reluctance to be vaccinated, use emotional IUIs in its PR campaign? Finally, could emotional interfaces *between* machines cooperate in their own emotion-shaping projects, without any human supervision?

For now, IUIs are simply interested in getting to know human emotion better, and in the connections between feeling and trust. We have touched on McLuhan's view that media is an extension of our personality, and on our so-far insatiable need to extend ourselves into media. Emotional IUIs are going to challenge our assumption that this is one-way process. They could extend *their* emotional capabilities into *our* selfhood, maybe driven by PR's need to manage trust between organisations and us, between celebrities and us, between the sources of authority in society and us. We won't be content to receive. If we have something to say to a wider community, we will extend ourselves into the IUIs. This might be a good thing. IUI's interconnections between emotion, trust, and action may encourage more people to communicate in civic affairs and commercial decisions, and at a much more detailed level than in the past. Emotional IUIs could encourage users by sharing feelings as well as data. They may become useful for 'the orderly functioning of group life' that Bernays, writing in 1928, believed PR had to encourage for the sake of social cohesion (Bernays, 2005, p. 38).

IUIs that can read our feelings at a deep level, and use them to build trust, might change public communication for the better. A lot depends on the motives of those who own or rent the IUIs, decide their objectives, and their place in PR. Paradoxically, emotional IUIs may give organisations a chance to present information more objectively, since a trusting individual might be open to more diverse data, liberated from the pressures of short-term volatile swings in public mood.

That too could be a good thing. There is enough evidence from this century and the one before to support the opinion of Gustave Le Bon (1841–1931) who studied the crowd phenomenon and in 1895 wrote 'Crowds, being incapable both of reflection and of reasoning, are devoid of the notion of improbability' (Le Bon, 2002, p. 35). Escaping from the capricious, contradictory noise of social media into a far more realistic, emotionally intelligent and equal relationship with issues and organisations may make us more tolerant of data and depth and other views. In this way, in the hands of PR, the foundations for trust in society may become more solid thanks to IUIs. More solid or, in the wrong hands, irretrievably undermined.

References

Accenture. (2014, December 18). *2015 Fjord trends*. Retrieved from https://www.slideshare.net/fjordnet/fjord-trends-2015-42825657/29-EMOTIONAL_INTERFACESFROM_COMMANDS_TO_CONVERSATION05FJORDSUGGESTSWith

Accenture Insurance Financial Services. (2015, July 16). Emotional interfaces: From commands to conversation. *Accenture.* Retrieved from https://insuranceblog.accenture.com/emotional-interfaces-from-commands-to-conversation

Atkinson, D. J., & Clark, M. H. (2013, March). Autonomous agents and human interpersonal trust: Can we engineer a human-machine social interface for trust? In *AAAI spring symposium: Trust and autonomous systems.* Retrieved from http://atkinsonlab.com/research/2013-ihmc-aaai-ss-13-07-dja.pdf

Bacinello, E., Carmona, L. J. D. M., Tomelim, J., Da Cunha, H. C., & Tontini, G. (2017). Nonlinear antecedents of consumer satisfaction on e-banking portals. *The Journal of Internet Banking and Commerce, 22*(S8), 1–21.

Bernays, E. L. (2005). *Propaganda*. New York: Ig.

Braun, M., Schubert, J., Pfleging, B., & Alt, F. (2019). Improving driver emotions with affective strategies. *Multimodal Technologies and Interaction, 3*(1), 21. Retrieved from file:///Users/Simon/Downloads/mti-03-00021.pdf

Clayton, D., & Jones, C. (2008, September 22). Emotion and voice user interfaces. *UX Matters.* Retrieved from https://www.uxmatters.com/mt/archives/2008/09/emotion-and-voice-user-interfaces.php

Esposito, A., Fortunati, L., & Lugano, G. (2014). Modeling emotion, behavior and context in socially believable robots and ICT interfaces. *Cognitive Computation, 6*(4), 623–627.

Fahr, R., & Irlenbusch, B. (2008). Identifying personality traits to enhance trust between organisations: An experimental approach. *Managerial and Decision Economics, 29*(6), 469–487.

Frison, A. K., Wintersberger, P., Riener, A., Schartmüller, C., Boyle, L. N., Miller, E., & Weigl, K. (2019, May). In UX we trust: Investigation of aesthetics and usability of driver-vehicle interfaces and their impact on the perception of automated driving. *Proceedings of the 2019 CHI conference on human factors in computing systems* (pp. 1–13). New York: Association for Computing Machinery.

Fruhling, A. L., & Lee, S. M. (2006). The influence of user interface usability on rural consumers' trust of e-health services. *International Journal of Electronic Healthcare, 2*(4), 305–321.

Garay-Vitoria, N., Cearreta, I., & Larraza-Mendiluze, E. (2019). Application of an ontology-based platform for developing affective interaction systems. *IEEE Access, 7*, 40503–40515. Retrieved from https://ieeexplore.ieee.org/stamp/stamp.jsp?arnumber=8662572

Garcia-Molina, G., Tsoneva, T., & Nijholt, A. (2013). Emotional brain–computer interfaces. *International Journal of Autonomous and Adaptive Communications Systems, 6*(1), 9–25.

Gooch, D., Vasalou, A., Benton, L., & Khaled, R. (2016, May). Using gamification to motivate students with dyslexia. *Proceedings of the 2016 CHI conference on human factors in computing systems* (pp. 969–980). ACM. Retrieved from https://pure.ulster.ac.uk/ws/files/77515044/TiiS_2019_Feb_009.R1.pdf (77pp).

Green, B. D. (2010). Applying human characteristics of trust to animated anthropomorphic software agents. (Order No. 3423463, State University of New York at Buffalo). *ProQuest Dissertations and Theses*, 326.

Hastie, H., Liu, X., & Patron, P. (2017, November). Trust triggers for multimodal command and control interfaces. *Proceedings of the 19th ACM international conference on multimodal interaction* (pp. 261–268). Retrieved from https://dl.acm.org/doi/pdf/10.1145/3136755.3136764?casa_token=RQhTcFJUN-F4AAAAA:NnxUUXjJIoFcXXyrm_mNfOz0fGlM1cVQ1esxnlRVUK-frZTSVdBcX4ij_WLJyF_paaZ-4CmQG4DVniA

Hawlitschek, F., Jansen, L. E., Lux, E., Teubner, T., & Weinhardt, C. (2016, January). Colors and trust: The influence of user interface design on trust and reciprocity. In *2016 49th Hawaii international conference on system sciences (HICSS)* (pp. 590–599). NJ: Piscataway IEEE.

Hayes-Roth, B., Ball, G., Lisetti, C., Picard, R. W., & Stern, A. (1998, January). Panel on affect and emotion in the user interface. *Proceedings of the 3rd international conference on Intelligent user interfaces* (pp. 91–94). New York: Association for Computing Machinery.

Hussein, T., Chauhan, P. K., Dalmer, N. K., Rudzicz, F., & Boger, J. (2020). Exploring interface design to support caregivers' needs and feelings of trust in online content. *Journal of Rehabilitation and Assistive Technologies Engineering, 7*, 2055668320968482.

Ihlen, Ø., & Verhoeven, P. (2012). A public relations identity for the 2010s. *Public Relations Inquiry, 1*(2), 159–176. Retrieved from https://journals.sagepub.com/doi/pdf/10.1177/2046147X11435083?casa_token=rEFFH-2SaqVUAAAAA:HMugK7K5oF7_XaKpM3XZKxz_WnmOqkVlbeTJ-FMiEEoQu4I2S6UPgcZ5WmR4EXAZ47Z-NSgEWGRyxg

Keser, C. (2003). Experimental games for the design of reputation management systems. *IBM Systems Journal, 42*(3), 498.

Khairuddin, I. E. (2019). Understanding and designing for trust in bitcoin blockchain. (Order No. 28277824, Lancaster University (United Kingdom)). *PQDT – Global*, 351. Retrieved from http://ezp.bentley.edu/login?url=https://www.proquest.com/dissertations-theses/understanding-designing-trust-bitcoin-blockchain/docview/2472190042/se-2?accountid=8576

Kim, S. E., & Arnett, K. P. (2012). Exploring satisfaction with the portal's "Cs": Assessing US and Korean preferences. *Internet Research*, 22(1), 75–97.

Kuznetsov, G. (2019, January 19). Designing emotional interfaces of the future. *Smashing Magazine*. Retrieved from https://www.smashingmagazine.com/2019/01/designing-emotional-interfaces-future/

Le Bon, G. (2002). *The crowd: A study of the popular mind*. Mineola, NY: Dover Publications.

Lugmayr, A. (2016, November). Emotive media: A review of emotional interfaces and media in human-computer-interaction. *Proceedings of the 28th Australian conference on computer-human interaction* (pp. 338–342). New York: Association of Computing Machinery. Retrieved from https://dl.acm.org/doi/pdf/10.1145/3010915.3010982?casa_token=t8n4zHCyp-i0AAAAA:GEh2f1M25mAYrtRxfrtb_pdvXqrQILCvhHbwl8uDaRon-Cw6zOiSyOEfjpDhPJ3ASoBsi2y3P4UKWbg

Mäkäräinen, M., Kätsyri, J., & Takala, T. (2014). Exaggerating facial expressions: A way to intensify emotion or a way to the uncanny valley? *Cognitive Computation*, 6(4), 708–721.

MIT. (2020). Affective computing. *MIT Media Lab*. Retrieved from https://affect.media.mit.edu/

MIT. (2021). Affective computing. Overview. *MIT Media Lab*. Retrieved from https://www.media.mit.edu/groups/affective-computing/overview/

Morris, R. R., Kouddous, K., Kshirsagar, R., & Schueller, S. M. (2018). Towards an artificially empathic conversational agent for mental health applications: System design and user perceptions. *Journal of Medical Internet Research*, 20(6), e10148.

Mynatt, E. D., Essa, I., & Rogers, W. (2000, November). Increasing the opportunities for aging in place. *Proceedings on the 2000 conference on universal usability* (pp. 65–71). New York: Association of Computing Machinery. Retrieved from https://dl.acm.org/doi/pdf/10.1145/355460.355475?casa_token=QhoOJOHO3ssAAAAA:fGI32sVQoDemyOz5iEHz5joG_yx-Dsc-Ln55tB7A5d8hEgFP5KRybn33BvIpByefr7JeavVUW02x

NBC. (2006, January 5). Walmart blames human error for offensive link. *NBC News*. Retrieved from https://www.nbcnews.com/id/wbna10730202

Norman, D. A., & Ortony, A. (2003, November). Designers and users: Two perspectives on emotion and design. *Proceedings of the symposium on foundations of interaction design* (pp. 1–13). Interaction Design Institute, Ivrea, Italy.

Norris, M. (2020, August 27). Brain-computer interfaces are coming. Will we be ready? Rand Corporation. Retrieved from https://www.rand.org/blog/

articles/2020/08/brain-computer-interfaces-are-coming-will-we-be-ready. html

Oh, S. Y., Bailenson, J., Krämer, N., & Li, B. (2016). Let the avatar brighten your smile: Effects of enhancing facial expressions in virtual environments. *PLoS ONE, 11*(9), 1–18. https://doi.org/10.1371/journal.pone.0161794

Priya, J. R., Anbarasu, A. J., & Xavier, S. (2017). The role of service evaluation index in the creation of emotional brands. *IUP Journal of Brand Management, 14*(3), 30–44. Retrieved from http://ezp.bentley. edu/login?url=https://www.proquest.com/scholarly-journals/role-service-evaluation-index-creation-emotional/docview/1953853103/ se-2?accountid=8576

Rawlins, B. L. (2007). Trust and PR practice. *Institute for Public Relations* [Online]. Retrieved from https://www.instituteforpr.org/wp-content/uploads/Rawlins-Trust-formatted-for-IPR-12-10.pdf

Rayport, J. F., & Jaworski, B. J. (2001). *E-commerce.* Boston, MA: McGraw-Hill Irwin.

Rochon, S. (2019, August 20). Artificial intelligences have emotions. *Becoming Human.* Retrieved from https://becominghuman.ai/artificial-intelligences-have-emotions-659cb09cdc61

Ruijten, P. A., Terken, J., & Chandramouli, S. N. (2018). Enhancing trust in autonomous vehicles through intelligent user interfaces that mimic human behavior. *Multimodal Technologies and Interaction, 2*(4), 62.

Sinha, R. (2006, January 10), When recommendations go bad: Walmart & the "Planet of the Apes" fiasco. *Rashmi's Blog.* Retrieved from https:// rashmisinha.com/2006/01/10/when-recommendations-go-bad-walmart-the-planet-of-the-apes-fiasco/

Valentini, C., & Kruckeberg, D. (2011). Public relations and trust in contemporary global society: A Luhmannian perspective of the role of public relations in enhancing trust among social systems. *Central European Journal of Communication, 4*(1), 91–107.

van der Heide, A., & Trivino, G. (2010, July). Simulating emotional personality in human computer interfaces. In *International conference on fuzzy systems* (pp. 1–7). IEEE. Retrieved from http://www.avdheide.nl/publications/ VanderHeide_Trivino_[2010]_Simulating_Emotional_Personality_in_ Human_Computer_Interfaces.pdf

Wang, R., Chen, L. L., & Solheim, I. (2019). Modeling Dyslexic Students' motivation for enhanced learning in e-learning systems. *ACM Transactions on Interactive Intelligent Systems,* 17–09. Retrieved from https://pure.ulster. ac.uk/ws/files/77515044/TiiS_2019_Feb_009.R1.pdf

Yu, K., Berkovsky, S., Taib, R., Conway, D., Zhou, J., & Chen, F. (2017, March). User trust dynamics: An investigation driven by differences in system performance. *Proceedings of the 22nd international conference on intelligent user interfaces* (pp. 307–317). New York: Association for Computing Machinery.

Zhang, L., Weitlauf, A. S., Amat, A. Z., Swanson, A., Warren, Z. E., & Sarkar, N. (2019). Assessing social communication and collaboration in autism spectrum disorder using intelligent collaborative virtual environments. *Journal of Autism and Developmental Disorders*, 50(1), 1–13.

Zhou, J., Luo, S., & Chen, F. (2020). Effects of personality traits on user trust in human–machine collaborations. *Journal on Multimodal User Interfaces*, *14*, 387–400. Retrieved from https://opus.lib.uts.edu.au/bitstream/10453/140753/2/uncertainty_CL_TML_JMUI_final.pdf

Zhou, T., & Lu, Y. (2011). The effects of personality traits on user acceptance of mobile commerce. *International Journal of Human-Computer Interaction*, *27*(6), 545–561. https://doi.org/10.1080/10447318.2011.555298

4 Just like us? Listening and learning interfaces

Listening like us, not looking like us

According to Sproull et al. (1996, p. 119), 'Many people want computers to be responsive to people. But do we also want people to be responsive to computers?' Sometimes we do, given the potential for co-operative and even negotiated working relationships between human and machine. This means IUIs have to be proactive as well, and that too makes them important to PR.

As we've suggested, it would be a blunder for PR to see IUIs simply as tools, and probably a historic blunder. IUIs try to engage us in ways that go beyond obtaining goods or services. 'Us' in this case means us as a target audience, or as representatives for an organisation, or even as PR practitioners navigating between the two. Looked at this way, an interface's relatability must involve successfully mimicking human traits that PR already works with, but not necessarily the most obvious ones of appearance or movement.

We have not talked much about attaching IUIs to humanlike faces or limbs. Robotic limbs and looks are in a sense a part of the interface, not apart from it: delivering, for example, an impression of strength or autonomy. It's a premise behind a good deal of science fiction. Whether or not it is a robot, an interface's best PR assets are naturally its communication assets, intended or accidental. These include IUI's ability to learn and listen (auditory UI). Humans might respond better to IUIs that seem to have senses much like ours; take in information in roughly the same ways as us, make judgements, and express themselves in roughly the same ways we do.

None of that means devices have to look like us, or that such a thing is achievable or welcome. New York City Police Department sent a robot dog back to the manufacturer and cancelled the contract after complaints about the cost and its 'creepy, alienating' appearance,

DOI: 10.4324/9781003111320-4

in the words of the Mayor's spokesperson (Bowman, 2021). Some new research does suggest that visual design works better than auditory design when trying to make products seem more human to consumers, and we might feel our personal experience confirms that (Yuan & Dennis, 2020). On the other hand, IUIs are not really designed as human faces, either static or with a pre-programmed repertoire of expressions. They are *inter*faces, made to manage an interchange between 'faces' of users and organisations, and the more unforced that interchange the better. They must interact with us for many reasons. In complex communication encounters facial sophistication doesn't matter as much as satisfactory communication, and 'increasing the "humanness" of an interface by adding more human qualities to it does not necessarily make people like it more' (Sproull et al., 1996, p. 99).

It's been said of robots, the most humanlike of intelligent artificial agents, that their success 'hinges not only on their utility, but also on their ability to be responsive to and interact with people in a natural and intuitive manner' (Breazeal, 2004, p. 181). Our affinity with devices including robots may be based more on how they absorb, exchange and express information from, with and to us. In other words, on the communication capabilities of the interface. Achieving a physical similarity to us is in any case hard to pull off. That is the challenging premise behind Masahiro Mori's 'uncanny valley'. Mori, a professor of robotics, coined the phrase in 1970 to chart the progression of robots towards a more human appearance, reaching a trough where appearance was puppet-like enough to arouse human discomfort – the uncanny valley – before better designs moved robots out of this trough and towards being more accepted.

We have scarcely begun to cross that valley. Mori understood that 'human beings themselves lie at the final goal of robotics' (Mori, 1970, p. 34), but until that could be successfully achieved, 'we predict that it is possible to produce a safe familiarity by a nonhumanlike design' (Mori, 1970, p. 34). There need be no valley to cross when communicating with an IUI. It need not be a human face and until robots have crossed the uncanny valley it may feel easier to work with a non-robot IUI skilled in communication.

Listening ability ranks high among those skills. What qualities should an auditory UI have? Among them must be the ability to hear what we're saying and draw relevant conclusions, adapting its conclusions to the situation. 'The interface should be able to handle potential problems of human speech such as sentence fragments, false starts, and interruptions' a research team recommended in 2001 (Perzanowski et al., 2001, p. 17). It should also be able to disambiguate (remove any ambiguity) and fill in all the references to the context including historical, geographical, and social. Today we're more familiar with such interfaces, which are now taking their first halting steps. Voice command interfaces are well established: cellphones with voice dictation, a smart speaker for the desk. Some listening interfaces are trying to diagnose our needs, frustrating as it can be for us. Take an automated customer service device listening as we answer its questions and either offering us more (and hopefully helpful) options, or directing us into a vortex in which the only escape is to hang up or try and find another human.

Other listening and learning IUIs want to join in more creatively, partnering with us in music, one of the most prized expressions of our individuality. Musicians and music lovers 'heavily rely on and benefit from intelligent approaches that enable users to access sound and music in unprecedented manners' including 'audio search and browsing interfaces; music learning interfaces; music recommender systems; machine learning for new digital musical instruments' (Knees et al., 2019, p. 11). Other listening interfaces are being developed to help aging in place, with speech and sound capabilities to manage appliances or lighting using speech wherever possible (Portet et al., 2013). And, not finally by any means, our computer can listen to us even when we're not talking to it. 'Most laptops' *PCWorld* noted in 2019, 'ship with "far field" capabilities specifically designed to pick up and recognise your voice at a distance, even across a crowded room' (Hachman, 2019).

A fully advanced listening IUI, incidentally, would presumably pass at least part of the original Turing Test, in which the machine's communication skills are indistinguishable from human communication skills, by hearing and understanding our questions well enough to reply as naturally as a human. If natural language is one feature required by such a machine, active listening must be another. Work on interfaces designed for elderly users reminds us that 'Active listening is a way of counseling that involves listening characterized by empathy, genuineness and warmth. It facilitates the client's understanding his/her own opinion and builds the client's self-confidence' (Kobayashi et al., 2010, p. 161). However, a 2020 investigation of interview chatbots reported 'few systems support the easy creation and customization of empathetic AI agents with active listening skills' (Xiao et al., 2020, p. 10). Success in Alan Turing's famous test, described in 1950, would therefore appear to rely on active listening and learning, not appearance. True, his test allowed the questioner to write the questions, but a better machine would convincingly cope with the nuances, speed, ambiguities and many imperfections of human speech, and on complex subjects. Robots with an active listening interface would be a big step in their journey across the uncanny valley.

Interfaces that can listen and divine the meaning, or meanings, of what is being said to them, and build on what is being said to them, would present PR with unexpected new media. In the words of one popular Twitter account 'screw it, put a chip in it. say hello' (Internet of shit, 2021). Perhaps PR should pay attention to vacuum cleaners. Listening is not just about an IUIs ability to understand nuance and ambiguity. As we've suggested, as far as PR is concerned a good IUI gives an impression of trust. It might, for instance, have familiar features which make a communication exchange more comfortable. It may be good at satisfying whatever the other user is looking for, or satisfactorily explaining why it can't be provided. For those reasons, successful IUIs will be placed in previously 'dumb' but comfortably familiar appliances. Will future PR practitioners be oblivious to the communication assets of, say, a vacuum, fridge or washing machine? Is there any reason why PR should ignore the fact that immersive technology is on the verge of making them into media? Actually, certain appliances are already able to listen to us. 'Could your vacuum be listening to you?' A University of Maryland news release asked about research which:

> Collected information from the laser-based navigation system in a popular vacuum robot and applied signal processing and deep learning techniques to recover speech and identify television programs playing in the same room as the device.
>
> (University of Maryland, 2020)

Needless to say, privacy issues are raised by the information about homes that vacuum bots store in the cloud, and by the possibility of attacking the vacuum via its Light Detection and Ranging (Lidar) sensors, and particularly its sound recordings (Sami et al., 2020). Would the listening, learning and perhaps one day talking abilities of robot vacuums tempt competing brands, nonprofit groups or the authorities? And if one organisation or government declines to use them in this way, would all the others do the same, seeking a communication advantage? To keep PR out of vacuum cleaners with an IUI, everyone would all have to agree to restrain themselves. A single holdout risks exposing the vacuum's owner to a communication monopoly – propaganda.

Let's admit that up to now PR has made little use of robot vacuum cleaners, which are in an early stage of development. The idea of treating them as media, as a receiver or transmitter of perceptions, seems absurd, which perhaps is part of the attraction. To discount something risks being unguarded about it. A robot vacuum might mediate our thoughts in our most unguarded moments which perhaps is what the prize of target audience 'authenticity' really means, in terms of strategic communication. On the premise that such 'authenticity' reveals the 'truth' about the individual expressing an opinion or desire, robot vacuums and other discounted devices may for a while number among the most powerful PR devices in the world, until we learn to treat them differently. What could PR do with them? The first possibility, because the technology is already in place, is clearly that their ability to collect information about a home increases the scope for engaging the homeowners based on their domestic aspirations or necessities, and constructing a product or company reputation that answers them by fitting far more closely with the individual's aspirations. Immersive technology like that may establish finely tuned communication relationships, able to observe and satisfy the individual in the right mood at the right moment.

If and when vacuums become a media platform, engaging with the individual in a private not shared sphere, why would public relations pay less attention to their potential than to any other media platform? The attractions of freely available information like this also suggest governments might occasionally be listening to robot vacuums too; possibly for security reasons, and possibly, later, for policy or electoral reasons, with implications for voting and party politics, managed persuasion or – for the already persuaded – opinion reinforcement and maintenance.

Imagine a domestic appliance that continuously reports information just as stock indexes report stocks. Organisations receive the information and invest in our opinions and preferences, enhancing their PR so that the attractions of a chosen interface can be brought into play. Its familiarity, domesticity, friendliness, simplicity, and its alertness and attentiveness to the user reinforces whatever we have told it to say.

Listening interfaces, then, can help organisations adapt their operations and their PR to what they hear. At the same time, learning interfaces are in development that may not need to work with the human senses, including listening. Some of those interfaces and their possible effect on strategic communication will be discussed in the next section, which deals with interfaces that learn.

Learning like us: natural, neural, heterogeneous

Simplicity is a virtue in strategic communication. So too is natural-ness, and interfaces that do not impose their version of a relationship upon users, preferring a more natural relationship, would presumably be useful and better at meeting some of the standards set by Turing and Mori. Natural interactions between interface and individual de-pend on machine learning as much as on imitating human senses. 'What we want' Alan Turing said in 1947, 'is a machine that learns from experience'. (Turing, 1995, p. 13). In this relatively early stage of development, machine learning is the search for useful patterns by supervision or trial and error, frequently supported by adaptive and artificial neural networks of chips and circuits driven by formulae mimicking (or trying to mimic) the brain's neurons, synapses, axons and dendrites.

Turing also believed that 'the machine must be allowed to have con-tact with human beings in order that it may adapt itself to their stand-ards' (Turing, 1995, p. 13), and recent research continues to emphasise this view: 'In order to perform complex tasks in realistic human en-vironments, robots need to be able to learn new concepts in the wild, incrementally, and through their interactions with humans' (Azagra et al., 2020, p. 1883). For those reasons, some of the robots made by the noted Australian roboticist Rodney Brooks were approximately human size so that they see the world similarly to us, which helps us interact with them more like we interact with humans. In this too, hu-man factors matter to interfaces as they do to public relations. An information exchange must take place, a decision must be reached, an action must be taken.

The US Department of Defense has raised the need for protocols in jointly led human-machine missions. Similar developments may be expected in medical procedures, and are to some extent established in games, based on mutual observation of rules when alternating be-tween human or machine interventions. Machines, like many humans, can have problems knowing what to do with new information or situa-tions, therefore 'robotic perception should have lifelong learning com-ponents' (Azagra et al., 2020, p. 1883). The goal of a more natural and co-operative working relationship between human and machine must include interfaces that adapt to machine learning.

To be of any use to PR, an IUI – for example, a game for children with learning difficulties that uses 'a natural user interactivity inter-face' (Chatzidaki et al., 2017, p. 20) – must learn and adjust to unpre-dictable decisions, gestures or movements by the user. The IUI must learn incrementally, on the spot and in the phrase just-quoted 'in the wild' (Azagra et al., 2020). In fluid, rapidly evolving situations interfaces must respond appropriately to be of use to public relations. They must react and adapt naturally, and whether they are robots or other devices the IUI that engages the individual most closely will preferably show that the device learns by heterogeneity, giving the impression of receiving information by multiple means – for instance, by sight, sound or touch; using sensors much as a human uses senses. Interfaces also need to learn their own limitations and know not to act in situations where they are not competent to do so. In such circumstances, they should, hopefully, defer to a human who, also hopefully, is better equipped to deal with the situation. That said, all these now-essential capabilities, some of which we've already explored, may one day be relegated to necessary special effects, as we shall shortly see.

Whatever its appearance, the IUI is ideally the face of a 'naturally' intelligent technology. In a way it is where many nerves in the technology's artificial nervous system are concentrated, as nerves might concentrate in our own sense organs. If we like it, or at least trust it, we will use learning to exploit the media potential of the interface. The IUIs of the future must express the personality and purpose of the machine, and link to the PR strategy of the organisation controlling it or paying to use it. Such an interface can't do PR properly unless it or the whole device is capable of socio-emotional intelligence. A leading robotics researcher has counselled: 'such characteristics cannot be restricted to the surface (at the "interface"), but integrated deep into the core of their [robot] design' (Breazeal, 2004, p. 185):

> Hence the functionality of the robot cannot be easily partitioned into 'interface' behavior, 'task' behavior, and 'survival' behavior. The social and emotive qualities of a robot serve not only to 'lubricate' the interface between itself and its human interlocutor, but also play a pragmatic role in promoting survival, self-maintenance, learning, decision-making, attention, and more.
>
> (Breazeal, 2004, p. 184)

It should be repeated that like a real PR practitioner (rather than the popular clichés of a practitioner), an IUI built for strategic communication must be able to listen and learn. It must be backed by substantial and trustworthy content from the organisation to build lasting, convincing relations with the target audience. It can't rely on listening, relaying the information into a void, and reproducing platitudes. The service it provides must be convincing, whether it is a product or a point of view. The IUI, like so many other new technologies, is a 'social intervention' (Frauenberger & Purgathofer, 2019, p. 58), and it socially intervenes by listening, learning and engaging in effective communication. Without those complementary skills, an interface cannot connect you to its device, and make you known to the organisations with a stake in the device. An IUI should be the newest extension of our minds, predicted by Marshal McLuhan, whose most quoted line, perhaps, is 'The Medium is the Message', a phrase which as it has turned out brilliantly fuses technology, communication, the individual and society into a message about our future as media devices (McLuhan & Gordon, 2013, Chapter 1). It must be mutually interesting to PR and IUIs that:

> 'the medium is the message' because it is the medium that shapes and controls the scale and form of human association and action.
> (McLuhan & Gordon, 2013, Chapter 1)

'Shapes and controls'. How far can IUIs shape and control interactions with humans? Could they eventually achieve communication objectives without the need to persuade humans? For now, two-way communication matters. Expressing ourselves with media depends on an interface, and perhaps in time an interface that can listen and learn about us without accessing any of our external senses, communicating with us in silence and without even movement. Alter Ego, a prototype under development at the MIT Media Lab, takes the form of a headset whose interface communicates by bone conduction and listens by capturing 'peripheral neural signals when internal speech articulators are volitionally and neurologically activated, during a user's internal articulation of words'. 'Externally observable movements' are unnecessary. No one else needs to hear what we are thinking, only Alter Ego (MIT Media Lab, Alter Ego, Overview).

Alter Ego is pure interface; all about learning, listening, informing persuading. Would it or its more efficient descendants affect PR? In conventional circumstances an interface like this could present new opportunities to marginalised audiences. It overthrows PR's existing relationship with its audience, and traditional ideas about audience identity, by taking the 'social' out of social media and substituting an approach more intimately tailored to the individual interface users. Alter Ego is our second reminder (after vacuum cleaners) that an effective interface is about the ears, mouth and mind of the machine. Convincing human features and movements could matter less to PR than the interface's other communication abilities.

Alter Ego wants access to our neurons to improve communication exchanges. Other research is investigating our potential as information storage units for devices, and if 'it may be possible to harness living neurons as a means of packing more information into a very small space' (MacKellar, 2019, p. 45), sidestepping the potential problem that one day we may reach storage limits on computer chips:

> In the future, the use of neuronal interface systems using a computer may even improve a person's cognitive functions, such as memory, reasoning speed or access to data. But caution and realism is necessary to avoid overstating or exaggerating possible uses.
>
> (Neuronal Interface Systems, 2019, p. 47)

Does this suggest the interface is an exoskeleton for the mind, or would our minds become the exoskeleton for an interface, and for organisations reaching us through it? Our neurons and the intelligent user interface depend on external stimuli in order to function. They may be supplemented by shared stimuli, opening a new level for learning, collaboration and understanding by blending human and machine. In this scenario, each side plays to each other's strengths: the human brain stores the information and the IUI retrieves it, either for us, or for itself, or perhaps for organisations seeking to understand (if that is the right word) our facts, experiences, perceptions. Neuronal interfaces could blur the distinction between human and machine. A paraplegic's brain may be able to move complex prosthetic devices and express higher order preferences; while on the other side of the narrowing communication spectrum a simulated brain, such as those being developed by the EU's Human Brain Project, may help robots learn faster and independently, 'almost like living creatures' (Human Brain Project, 2020).

'The Brain Initiative' is a US government-backed project launched in 2013, which seeks 'to discover the patterns of neural activity and underlying circuit mechanisms that mediate mental and behavioural processes, including perception, memory, learning, planning, emotion, and complex thought' (NIH, 2020b, Section I). The stated purpose is to be able to understand and treat neurological disorders, but would that be enough to satisfy the opportunities for consciousness and autonomy raised by The Brain Initiative and the Human Brain Project, both of which will involve neuronal IUIs? In January a Chinese university and hospital announced a brain-computer interface (BCI) implant on a 72-year-old patient, paralyzed from the neck down, to help him control a mechanical arm with signals from his brain (China Daily, 2020). If, one day, a quadriplegic person can express himself to a far greater extent, and make more independent choices, will organisations use PR to supply him with persuasive reasons to make particular choices, using the same interfaces he uses to communicate with the world?

Amid these advances, with interfaces that can learn about our desires and our nervous system as well, it may seem trivial to ask how PR is affected by this. It isn't trivial. PR is omnipresent where groups gather to persuade and perceive. Strategic communication cannot overlook the fact that as we extend ourselves through such interfaces, which are essentially media for handling information, the media is extending itself further into our biochemistry. Who then will be in charge of whom? Does it even matter who is in charge? Will the categories of human and machine be redefined? Could the PR audience in an age of IUIs become a hybrid of organic and inorganic interfaces? The idea is unsettling, but a glance at history shows that new technologies for large-scale communication are rarely rejected. In this case neuronal IUIs might be used first by people with severe physical or mental challenges. A BCI might be used – as noted earlier – 'for restoring volitional control of external devices to patients paralyzed by injuries or strokes' (NIH, 2020a, Appendix A). Then the same technology is adapted by groups or individuals identifying other possibilities and using BCIs for their own private or public purposes in government, education, marketing, crisis or reputation management, entertainment and other forms of commerce. And also in defence: in March, 2018 the US Defense Advanced Research Projects Agency (DARPA) launched a Next-Generation Nonsurgical Neurotechnology (N^3) program 'to develop high-performance, bi-directional brain-machine interfaces for able-bodied service members'. The envisioned non-invasive technology combines 'to interface to multiple points in the brain at once' and:

> breaks through the limitations of existing technology by delivering an integrated device that does not require surgical implantation, but has the precision to read from and write to 16 independent channels within a $16mm^3$ volume of neural tissue within 50ms [milliseconds]
>
> (Emondi, 2020, Next Generation)

These interfaces could achieve a high degree of integration with users if they can access our nervous system, and are equipped to learn, listen and understand our innermost intentions. Would the neuronal connection between interface and human lessen the need for IUIs that work through our external physical senses, like hearing or touching? Since PR needs our external senses to influence an audience, would neuronal interfaces in the end reduce the need for PR?

PR inside the mind

Probably not. Not as long as organisations seek audiences and have to learn about them. Learning enables us to create, analyse, decide and act. The interfaces must also be managed and owned by people. Interfaces able to listen, understand, learn from the information they hear or receive by other means changes an IUI from a PR-owned platform to a PR partner independently managing relations with the targeted individuals. This is the latest iteration of a pattern in managed public communication that probably started with the earliest pre-modern media, where the media platform itself steadily became more potent at the expense of the intended message.

A collaborative, negotiated relationship between organisation, IUI, PR and target audiences is inevitable, if IUIs are not to use listening and learning to command and control. There are reasons to be hopeful about the prospects for this relationship. After all, machine learning seeks 'to focus on interaction and user interface issues in designing intelligent systems that learn from their users' (Amershi et al., 2013, p. 121). The primary purpose of interfaces remains to serve us. PR participation is a sign that human-centred priorities matter.

There are other reasons to feel hopeful. Humans are in principle alert to the dangers of intelligent interfaces. The perils of intellectually advanced devices have not escaped observers from the time that the Czech playwright Karel Čapek wrote and published *RUR (Rossum's Universal Robots)* in 1920. Čapek warned of humanoid devices with crude humanlike senses, some learning abilities, a dangerous unswerving attachment to their original purpose, and was the person who named them robots.

Interface designers understandably want to show us how their devices help people. PR however operates in ambiguous situations. It wants to know which IUIs can attract and influence individuals and through them society. Because of that, it is important that the methods used in PR must be understood by interface designers. PR works with many other kinds of interfaces: social media, news releases, meetings, experts. The need for interfaces is not going away. If interfaces vanished, organisations would become less visible. Organisations need interfaces to show themselves. For that reason, the interface and its biases must also be known to all. Fake news makes this requirement more urgent. The interface is like a clock (itself an interface of course); it can unobtrusively give us the data we need to make decisions, but unlike the clockmaker the people responsible for the interface must be known to us. Interface users need the interface to be as transparent with them as they are with it. Both sides of the encounter must listen and learn from each other. We will depend on interfaces as citizens to decide if we like, trust, cooperate and want what is being offered. On the other side of the interface, as a member of the communicating organisation, we have goods, services, ideas to communicate. In both identities we must understand how IUIs can affect our identity and reputation. PR practitioners will be listening and learning too. Those practitioners should have more technological or scientific knowledge than their professional predecessors: more knowledge of the interconnections between human and machine. PR's continued presence will show that a relatively equal relationship between user and interface remains important, and that humans have enough autonomy to reject command and control communications and make their own choices, hopefully in a still-private mental space of their own.

References

Amershi, S., Cakmak, M., Knox, W. B., Kulesza, T., & Lau, T. (2013, March). IUI workshop on interactive machine learning. *Proceedings of the companion publication of the 2013 international conference on Intelligent user interfaces companion* (pp. 121–124). New York: Association for Computing Machinery.

Azagra, P., Civera, J., & Murillo, A. C. (2020). Incremental learning of object models from natural human-robot interactions. *IEEE Transactions on Automation Science and Engineering, 17*(4), 1883–1900.

Bowman, E. (2021, April 30). 'Creepy' Robot Dog loses job with New York Police Department. NPR news. Retrieved from https://www.npr.org/2021/04/30/992551579/creepy-robot-dog-loses-job-with-new-york-police-department

Breazeal, C. (2004). Social interactions in HRI: The robot view. *IEEE Transactions on Systems, Man, and Cybernetics, Part C (Applications and Reviews), 34*(2), 181–186. Retrieved from http://rit.kaist.ac.kr/home/EE788LN?action=AttachFile&do=get&target=5.2_Social_interactions_in_HRI_the_robot_view_Breazea_3.pdf

Chatzidaki, E., Xenos, M., & Machaira, C. (2017, November). A natural user interface game for the evaluation of children with learning difficulties. In *WOCCI* (pp. 17–22). Retrieved from https://www.ceid.upatras.gr/webpages/faculty/xenos/papers/C116.pdf

China Daily. (2020, January 18). Implants give paralyzed man's brain new control. Retrieved from http://www.cdpf.org.cn/english/MediaCenter/updates2/202001/t20200119_673476.shtml

Emondi, A. (2020). *Next-generation nonsurgical neurotechnology*. DARPA. Retrieved from December 1 https://www.darpa.mil/program/next-generation-nonsurgical-neurotechnology

Frauenberger, C., & Purgathofer, P. (2019). Ways of thinking in informatics. *Communications of the ACM, 62*(7), 58–64. https://doi.org/10.1145/3329674

Hachman, M. (2019, June 27). Why your laptop's always-listening microphone should be as easy to block as your webcam. *PCWorld*. Retrieved from https://www.pcworld.com/article/3393254/computer-privacy-why-your-laptops-microphone-should-be-easier-to-block.html

Human Brain Project. (2020). *Robots*. Retrieved from November 30 https://www.humanbrainproject.eu/en/robots/

Internet of Shit. (2021). Retrieved https://twitter.com/internetofshit

Knees, P., Schedl, M., & Fiebrink, R. (2019, March). Intelligent music interfaces for listening and creation. *Proceedings of the 24th international conference on intelligent user interfaces: Companion* (pp. 135–136). New York: Association for Computing Machinery.

Kobayashi, Y., Yamamoto, D., Koga, T., Yokoyama, S., & Doi, M. (2010, March). Design targeting voice interface robot capable of active listening. In *2010 5th ACM/IEEE international conference on human-robot interaction (HRI)* (pp. 161–162). New York: Association for Computing Machinery.

McLuhan, M., & Gordon, W. T. (2013). *Understanding media: The extensions of man*. E-book. New York: Gingko Press. First published 1964.

MIT Media Lab. (2020). *Alter Ego, Overview*. Retrieved from November 26 https://www.media.mit.edu/projects/alterego/overview/

Mori, M. (1970). The uncanny valley. *Energy* (K. F. MacDorman and T. Minato, Trans), *7*(4), 33–35.

MacKellar C. (2019), *Cyborg mind: What brain–computer and mind–cyberspace interfaces mean for cyberneuroethics*. New York and Oxford: Berghahn Books. https://doi.org/10.2307/j.ctvvb7mw5.8

NIH. (2020a). *The brain initiative*. Appendix A. Retrieved from December 1 https://braininitiative.nih.gov/strategic-planning/brain-2025-report

NIH. (2020b). *The brain initiative*. Section I. The brain initiative: Vision and philosophy. Retrieved from December 1 https://braininitiative.nih.gov/strategic-planning/brain-2025-report

Perzanowski, D., Schultz, A. C., Adams, W., Marsh, E., & Bugajska, M. (2001). Building a multimodal human-robot interface. *IEEE Intelligent Systems, 16*(1), 16–21. Retrieved from https://apps.dtic.mil/sti/pdfs/ADA434941.pdf

Portet, F., Vacher, M., Golanski, C., Roux, C., & Meillon, B. (2013). Design and evaluation of a smart home voice interface for the elderly: Acceptability and objection aspects. *Personal and Ubiquitous Computing, 17*(1), 127–144.

Sami, S., Dai, Y., Tan, S. R. X., Roy, N., & Han, J. (2020, November). Spying with your robot vacuum cleaner: Eavesdropping via lidar sensors. *Proceedings of the 18th conference on embedded networked sensor systems* (pp. 354–367).

Retrieved from https://dl.acm.org/doi/pdf/10.1145/3384419.3430781?casa_
token=DZlAkIhGoWUAAAAA:fFJ2oy-pjB6sbqumVqKJ1diH8lRs2Nny-
JWQhdisz0ruLrX44SUR5MSrZge2KL7QEAy_siZFMiIE8GA

Sproull, L., Subramani, M., Kiesler, S., Walker, J. H., & Waters, K. (1996).
When the interface is a face. *Human–Computer Interaction, 11*(2), 97–124.
Retrieved from http://www.cs.cmu.edu/afs/cs.cmu.edu/Web/People/kiesler/
publications/1996pdfs/1996_When-the-Interface-is-a-Face_hci.pdf

Turing, A. M. (1950). Computing machinery and intelligence. *Mind, 59*(236),
433–460.

Turing, A. M. (1995). Lecture to the London Mathematical Society on
20 February 1947. *MD Computing, 12*, 390. Retrieved from https://www.
vordenker.de/downloads/turing-vorlesung.pdf

University of Maryland. (2020, November 17). *Could your vacuum cleaner
be listening to you?* [Press release]. Retrieved https://cmns.umd.edu/
news-events/features/4699

Xiao, Z., Zhou, M. X., Chen, W., Yang, H., & Chi, C. (2020, April). If I hear
you correctly: Building and evaluating interview chatbots with active listening skills. *Proceedings of the 2020 CHI conference on human factors
in computing systems* (pp. 1–14). New York: Association for Computing
Machinery.

Yuan, L. (Ivy) & Dennis, A. R. (2020). Acting like humans? Anthropomorphism and consumer's willingness to pay in electronic commerce. *Journal
of Management Information Systems, 37*(2), 450–477. https://doi.org/10.1080
/07421222.2019.1598691

5   From talking to persuasion

Obstacles and opportunities

Obstacles and opportunities

Haptic interfaces and graphical user interfaces (GUIs) can be persuasive, as we've seen, but verbal persuasion promises the give and take of natural conversation to steer data and feeling. What would it take for a talking IUI to be persuasive enough for PR? We have Siri, Alexa or cuddly toys that can talk and (usually) carry out certain instructions but an IUI that understands and converses or negotiates with us in a completely natural, adaptable voice of its own is possibly further off for PR's purposes than IUIs with advanced haptics and graphics, and maybe brain-computer interfaces. That doesn't mean PR should ignore the subject. Computer science hasn't: 'Captology' is the acronym for Computers as Persuasive Technology, and has been studied since the 1990s (Fogg, 2003).

One scientific challenge is for IUIs to understand the *art* of persuasion. It's useful to remember that the ingredients are manifold, and closely connected to our emotions. For Aristotle in *Art of Rhetoric*, passions whether positive or negative, mild or strong, are the active agents 'on account of which people, undergoing a change, differ in the judgments they make' (Aristotle & Bartlett, 2019, Book 2, p. 77). Interface designers know 'emotional elements (either on persuader or persuadee side) can be used to increase or diminish the persuasiveness of a message' (Guerini et al., 2011, p. 562). The challenge to design is that persuasion and emotion are subjective experiences. We can differ in our responses to persuasion, between and within ourselves, because our encounters with emotion and information differ. We understand a message differently depending on our feelings about the subject communicated, on the communicator, and on other factors intrinsic to time, place and personality.

Perceptions of persuasion vary. Ideally, humans must feel they're being helped, not led, to a decision but sometimes persuasion comes

DOI: 10.4324/9781003111320-5

across as a command and help feels like control. It might still be agreed though that help and control are different things, and also persuading and commanding. It might be agreed that helping and persuading can cooperate in a persuasive process and that our perception of both is affected by how information is communicated in a particular situation, and by our mood, wishes or needs. With all these variables we continue to see persuasion and command as distinct concepts, and we think we know the difference.

Will IUIs know the difference? How will they navigate that shifting ground between helping and persuading and commanding and controlling? PR will need IUIs to encourage us to courses of action which we want to take or are reluctant about taking. What would persuasive IUIs need to be useful in PR? Aristotle recommends several hard to capture qualities: ethos (credibility), logos (reason), and pathos (emotion), and strategically managed communication is about all three, plus kairos (timing). But IUIs are the products of science and technology, which is not always comfortable with such subjects. Eminent physicist David Bohm (1917–1992) declared 'If something is right, you don't need to be persuaded. If somebody has to persuade you, then there is probably some doubt about it'. Persuasion is 'not really coherent or rational' (Bohm, 1996, p. 31). Bohm advocated 'dialogue' which 'is not to analyze things, or to win an argument, or to exchange opinions' but to 'listen to everybody's opinions':

> We can just simply share the appreciation of the meanings; and out of this whole thing, truth emerges unannounced – not that we have chosen it.
>
> (Bohm, 1996, p. 32)

Bohm assumes a division between truth and untruth, a situation that doesn't always exist. In the words of the preface to the University of Chicago's edition of *Art of Rhetoric*:

> When there is no objective truth to strive to find, all becomes the hegemony of this or that "discourse," which can be distinguished by its persuasive power but not by its access to the truth.
>
> (R.C. Bartlett in Aristotle & Bartelett, 2019, Preface, p. 10)

Do distinctions between truth and untruth, and persuasion or command matter to an IUI? An IUI 'that aims at inducing the user, or in general, the audience, to perform a specific action in the real world' (Guerini et al., 2011, p. 559) is an IUI doing public relations. In that situation, given shared goals between the IUI and the person as well as a user model of the person, PR-oriented IUIs should be good to go, at least in principle. The problem for PR practitioners is that the persuasive (or 'inducing') IUI may have no insights about the truth of a proposition however good its conversation and general usability, however much human users like David Bohm desire a truth to guide their actions.

It is also undeniable that incoherence and non-rationality are assets in PR persuasion, as are their opposites. Also useful (if not always used) are prudence, virtue and goodwill, the qualities necessary for credibility according to Aristotle (Aristotle & Bartlett, 2019, Book 2, p. 77). They are necessary because in PR a product or reputation, while it might have a 'truth' to convey, isn't always convincingly 'truer' than its rival product, or an alternative view of a crisis or issue. All sides in a debate may contain selections of truths and untruths, or are incomplete in some other way. PR must persuade people towards one side over one or more alternatives, each with something to be said for them. As they start participating in these often non-binary communication activities IUIs will need to help people make relative choices, when the right choice is not the same as a socially-approved or officially True choice. Informatics researchers developing a natural language system to encourage healthy eating decided that:

> Attempting to persuade the population to adopt more appropriate habits by employing only 'rational' and 'scientific' arguments is probably not effective: this is one of the domains in which mingling of rational and emotional strategies is justified.
> (Mazzotta et al., 2007, p. 42)

Interface research tries to understand these less tangible qualities of persuasion, which must accommodate multiple possible truths, since 'Future intelligent systems may have contextual goals to pursue that aims at inducing the user, or in general, the audience, to perform a specific action in the real world' (Guerini et al., 2011, p. 559). Some projects build on Aristotle's analysis by breaking persuasion down into its prime elements. One computer science paper, for example, identified six persuasion strategies and applied them to different cultural groups, and 'collectivists' and 'individualists'. It found that collectivists were more susceptible to persuasion strategies than individualists (Orji, 2016, p. 30), which supports the experiences of other observers from Classical Greece down to the present generation of politicians, brand managers and PR practitioners. It is one reason why groups are cultivated and if need be invented by PR and the organizations it works for.

Nevertheless, the next generation of IUIs could make PR more 'individualist'; less reliant on group identities, but still needing to persuade large numbers of people. Historically, technology has helped us express and multiply our identities. The division of identities is a by-product of surplus wealth and choice, and parallels the division of labour and knowledge. A capacity for intense personalisation means more division of identities. IUIs will destabilise some identities or reduce the authority of others with consequences for PR and persuasion. They might do that by suggesting, guiding or – more debatably – 'nudging' (defining alternative choices in a pseudo-objective way and favourably weighting one of them). In other words, in the hands of PR, persuasive interfaces could radically and rapidly change our sense of self. This is why, if we really want PR interfaces to be persuasive *and* helpful, we must be allowed to persuade back, to criticise and to counter the IUI. IUIs must in turn know how to compromise or concede.

On top of all these rather nebulous matters, very problematically for IUIs in PR, is the tendency among humans to change their minds. Machiavelli puts the PR problem well in *The Prince* (1513):

> The nature of the people is variable, and whilst it is easy to persuade them, it is difficult to fix them in that persuasion.
>
> (Machiavelli, 1992, p. 26)

A fully persuasive IUI must not only be alert to our caprices, it must know how to fix them in place. The 'fixing' process has special needs of its own.

Persuasive interfaces in PR

Subjective qualities of persuasion, emotion, the individualisation of media, and human changeability suggest that persuasive PR-friendly IUIs will learn several roles, from assisting to advising and teaching, to collaborating and perhaps – more problematically – to leading, as a medium's 'persuasiveness' is usually grown by a rebalancing in power between it and human users. In the case of talking IUIs the change is unwittingly led by research with no interest in strategic communication. Whatever our feelings about the ethical principles involved in this research, history suggests that strategic communicators will work with persuasive IUIs. Either the services that persuasive IUIs will offer will be too crucial or desirable for us to ignore, or we will recognise the authority of the interface. The latter possibility is, for example, indicated by an attempt to design an IUI to encourage healthy eating.

Whatever the age or gender, the findings suggested that, especially for people less inclined to be persuaded, 'Authority messages were preferred to other message types' (Josekutty Thomas et al., 2017, p. 84). 'Authority' in this case refers to *authoritative* messages backed with credible expert knowledge, as opposed to persuasion based on encouraging commitment and consistency, consensus, and liking (p. 83). There are on occasion times when we want decisions to be made for us, and to submit to them without argument.

Assisting

The prospects for interface persuasiveness, and what it might mean for PR, are becoming visible in Voice User Interfaces (VUIs) – interfaces capable of voice recognition and/or with voices of their own, and their evolution into Conversational User Interfaces (CUIs). UXPin, a User Experience design platform (UX or User Experience develops interfaces that best help humans navigate technologies) overly enthusiastically declared that 'In the world that's emerging, there is little room for any other interface other than sound'. There may be wider agreement for its next comment: 'The immediacy and versatility of voice form a direct link from user desire to device response' (UXPin, 2021).

Because of that link, VUIs are developing a relationship with its human users that PR has cultivated for a long time. When it comes to persuasion VUIs have several advantages over graphics, haptics or virtual reality. They don't need users to change their posture, strain eyes or use fingers. They are less distracting and safer for a person steering a car or running through the woods. For PR's own target audiences, listening and talking may also require less effort in a persuasive process than looking or touching. A highly persuasive voice and conversational vocabulary might be well-equipped to communicate complex and many-sided subjects. In the words of a tech writer 'A personable VUI also helps to increase brand affinity – you're more likely to use a particular device or service if it's more entertaining and ultimately more "human" in nature' (Requejo, 2018, p. 3).

In 1996 the possibilities for 'Computers as assistants' were foreshadowed in an influential book of the same name (Hoschka, 1996), and later developments have theoretically adhered to this idea. 'At this point in voice user interface history' a veteran VUI developer wrote in 2018, 'most conversations seem to be command-and-control requests. The user asks (or tells) the computer something, and the computer responds with an answer or comment' (Rolandi, 2018, p. 5). VUIs like that are often called 'digital personal assistants' (DPAs), or 'virtual butlers' (Trappl, 2013) designed as robots or other devices which are 'always on and always present' (Payr, 2013, p. 29). DPAs follow the instructions of users or – the next step – help them make simple choices in entertainment or domestic living. Well-known DPAs include Google Assistant which is 'ready to help when and where you need it' (Google Play, 2020). Alexa 'is designed to make your life easier' (Microsoft, 2020). Siri makes a virtue of anticipating its owner and 'does more than ever. Even before you ask' (Apple Siri, 2020).

Most of the time, these assistants are not capable of holding a conversation consisting of more than one turn, since they are not very good at using references to the current context. By turn we simply mean that you say something and then Siri answers. By reference to the current context we mean something like 'what's the weather today?' Siri answers and then we ask 'what about tomorrow?' referring to the implicit 'weather' but not saying the word. Virtual assistants can understand some of the simpler contexts, but not the nontrivial ones.

If PR adapts VUIs for its own purposes, would 'assistants' be an accurate or ethical description of the functions and relationship? Would the transition from assistants to something else happen almost without our noticing it? 'We propose', write the authors of a recent paper, 'that DPAs can be designed to have the power to persuade people to increase their daily exercise' (Paay et al., 2020, p. 2). Is a DPA that 'offers suggestions at opportune moments' or that 'can enable people to change their attitudes or behaviour in the real world' or which uses praise to 'lead users to be more open to persuasion' (Paay et al., 2020, p. 3) the same as a DPA that turns lights on and off or plays music when instructed? Or is it something else, something which could recommend a work-out routine for us, or pick a product or policy for us? What DPAs like that are *not*, is impartial. They have purposes, objectives, and now programmed preferences. If they can persuade us to adopt their point of view, they are on the way to becoming PR practitioners.

This trend is indirectly expressed by VUI research that wants to understand the reasons why some interfaces are used by humans, rather than the intrinsic structure of persuasion and the objectives of the organisation behind the interface. One group examined VUIs in smartphones by looking at 'usage patterns' or the user's own intentions which was defined as 'looking up, learning and leisure'. Our learning and leisure requirements enlarge the role of persuasion. They take communication beyond the 'request/response design' needed for DPAs (Porcheron et al., 2018, p. 9) and towards 'more inclusive and diverse interactions with technologies' (Kendall et al., 2020, p. 587).

Partnering and teaching

Hoschka's 1996 discussion of computers as assistants raised the need for computers to support and coordinate group activities, and develop mediating systems for supporting discussion, arguments and decisions. Interfaces involved in those activities are potentially moving beyond the request/response conception of assisting. What are they moving towards? One step towards 'partnership' not 'assistantship' is the development of mediating systems, and 'to naturally and painlessly reveal the powers of a voice user interface' (Rolandi, 2018, p. 5) by making affective (emotion-capable) computing better at recognising speech emotion (Kompella, 2021, p. 14). When a VUI responds to a human instruction it is an assistant. When it encourages a human to perform an essential function, sometimes without needing to be told, by reading emotional inflection, it is on the way to being a partner. In 2016 Omnicon Health Group, a large strategic communication and marketing company, forecast that a user's Voice Recognition and Voice Activated Technologies:

> Will now be empowered to request medical assistance and transportation, receive medication reminders, have access to their own doctor's advice and rehab instructions, as well as connect to home-automation devices.
>
> (Omnicon Health Group, 2016)

Like several of the interfaces described in this book, it is easy to see the value of assistive VUIs to housebound people, people with a high degree of autism, dementia patients or the disabled. Seen in purely communication terms, anyone using them can play a bigger part in the public sphere. There would be less need for others to advocate for them, less need to be confined in the identity of a 'patient' trying to satisfy immediate physical needs. People who live more independently thanks to VUIs can intervene more often on more topics. They will be more influential. VUIs would expand their activities and offer more choices. They will transition from a request/response assistant into a persuader and advocate. Some research, for instance, uses 'Vehicle Voice Agents' to persuade drivers to adopt eco-driving habits, finding among other things that 'Happy participants performed better on eco-driving when they were exposed to egoistic appeals than to altruistic appeals' (Joo & Lee, 2014, p. 255). Others have explored a combination of voice and movement in an avatar, to 'encourage and persuade learners to increase effort' (Chen et al., 2012, p. 63). Experiments have been made with 'social dialogue' or the interplay of negotiation and information between humans and computer-generated 'Conversational Agents' (e.g. Schulman & Bickmore, 2009; Shalyminov et al., 2018).

Other possibilities are coming that PR won't be able to avoid. VUIs offering encouragement and advice are 'influencers'. They shape choices with a judicious blend of emotion and data. They resemble human influencers online or elsewhere, and so become important to PR as an audience in their own right. Could PR work with such VUIs to encourage particular actions and preferences? Their attractions will grow for PR practitioners and target audiences if the VUI is embedded in the private world of a human target; a familiar part of the home in an internet of things. And if a VUI wants to persuade key audiences to do something, would or should PR permit reciprocal compromise in the interface itself, turning it into a form of audience as well as a media platform? The VUI influencer might also matter to PR as a gatekeeper to other media. It could become the interface between us and *all* our technology and the people behind them. 'Does it not make sense', asked an Amazon UX designer, 'to have one device that we wear, that connects your voice to all your smart devices?' (Thomas, 2017).

Leading and its consequences

The next stage for persuasive VUIs is the ability to choose subjects and the solutions, to encourage our participation, and gradually reverse roles in the request/response connection, from human request and machine response to machine request and human response. This needs IUIs that are better at conversation, making them more successful CUIs (Conversational User Interfaces). 'Instead of relying on existing interaction methods from web or mobile interfaces', wrote the editors of *Conversational UX Design*, a wide-ranging study:

> UX designers should be creating new kinds of methods that are native to conversational interfaces. As conversational UX design matures, we expect to see the establishment of standards for dialogue management, conversation sequencing and turn-taking.
> (Moore & Arar, 2018, p. 15)

The better interfaces get at conversation, the more persuasive they could be, and the better they can steer us or make our choices, turning them into highly effective (and 'affective' in terms of emotional awareness) PUIs (Persuasive User Interfaces). PUIs could decide many of the subjects we want to make choices in by spotlighting particular arguments, data, and examples, as PR and social and other media does today, and by exploiting their own design attractions, also as media can do today. PUIs could move interfaces from being partners to being leaders, which would make them vital to PR as a manager of human audiences.

That transition depends on how far the interface's persuasive abilities can develop, and if it is indeed the most effective way to use voice technology. Currently, less advanced versions of Conversational User Interfaces (like a text-messaging Chatbot or a voice interface) are trying to bring brands, celebrities, influencers, politicians, campaigners, or corporations closer to the user, by adjusting to vocabulary, emotions, and pronunciation. UX Designers are seeking ways to 'hook users' to more persuasive interfaces. Among the hooks UXPin explicitly recommends are feedback loops, *kairos* (choosing the right moment), timely triggers or nudges, tailoring to user preferences, and creating recurring events to build anticipation or sustained interest or simply comfort in the interface (Toxboe, 2020). Another hook is attraction, which may eventually involve a human-looking interface, or more imminently an aesthetically pleasing and usable design. The director of Stanford University's Behavior Design Lab (formerly the Persuasive Technology Lab) has observed 'If interactive faces are to be used for persuasive purposes, such as counselling, training, or advertising, they need to be visually pleasing to be most effective' (Fogg, 2002, p. 93). So many hooks; persuasive interface designers have much more to learn about them. If they learn well enough, PR practitioners might come to the public arena with interfaces capable of the same subjective shortcuts as humans. If this happens, as we have said earlier, it would be sensible to ensure that the interfaces know when to stop and concede a point, and the threshold between persuasion and compulsion. Persuasion contains elements of negotiation. If an interface can't tell the different between a concession and a defeat, it undermines its powers of persuasion, retaining only the fig leaf of the word itself, covering a reality of compulsion.

Could humans accept a change in the interface from assistant to partner and then leader? A lot depends on how we perceive IUI leadership. Acceptance could, for instance, grow from seeing persuasive interfaces as helpful and important for the resolution of problems we agree on; encouraging us in those moments when we want to be talked into doing the right thing. The title of graduate thesis at Australia's Deakin University provides an example: "Evaluating Persuasive User Interfaces for Online Help-Seeking for Domestic Violence" (Singh, 2018). An interface that helps someone in trouble get help uses persuasion differently than an IUI asking us to believe something about a brand or person. How insistent should we let interface persuasion become if it's for a good cause? In the domestic abuse example, very insistent IUI persuasion seems justified.

A shade more ambiguously but no less significantly, other research has raised 'the challenging and relatively unexplored research space of *implicitly persuasive UI design*' (their italics) (Seering et al., 2019, p. 2). The team created graphic and text interfaces 'designed with the intention to persuade users to change their way of thinking or behaving' (p. 3), in this case by 'priming' (preparing) audience emotions and attentiveness to improve civil discourse in online commenting. The authors produced a particularly thought-provoking paper which accepted:

> The possibility that priming can be used for unscrupulous purposes. While this is already happening with great frequency in the deployment of online political propaganda, targeted marketing campaigns, spambots, and the like. – [sic] one can argue that our work provides even more specific guidelines for *designing effective priming methods to achieve desired persuasive ends.* [our italics]
>
> (Seering et al., 2019, p. 11)

However:

> While priming can temporarily change emotional states, behaviors, and goals, it is not an effective means of inducing individuals to engage in counterattitudinal behaviors or to endorse beliefs or actions that are not already within their latitude of acceptance.
>
> (Seering et al., 2019, p. 12)

The last statement seems debatable. People often engage in 'counterattitudinal behaviour' and change their public communication to justify that new behaviour, whatever their original reservations. We cannot overlook that and other long-term impacts of one-way priming. One result might be the cancelling of alternative views. There are other dangers: an overriding attraction to the interface design, a confusion of medium with message, an intolerant certainty in our own preferences, and the fact that irreversible long-term damage could be inflicted on a person or organisation in the heat of a well-primed moment.

How much of our future with persuasive IUIs depends on proofing ourselves with qualities that are now under tremendous pressure or ignored altogether in public discourse? Wisdom instead of smartness, perspective over persuasion? One test is to ask ourselves if we would tolerate interfaces nudging and priming for things we agree with, looking the other way when organisations we support use those methods.

Could we tolerate the same methods from competing products or views? Or would we try to shut them down and drift into a monopoly of persuasion that in the end is not persuasion at all? Should designers of persuasive IUIs look further than persuasion itself? Is being persuasive the same as being wise? Or is wisdom itself just another relative term on the dissecting table of empirical research: absolute as an idea, but in practice unhelpful, many-faceted and prey to an IUI's hooks, priming, nudges, and emotional exploitations? Maybe this is a good place to mention dark patterns. These are design patterns that use a deep understanding of users to trick them into doing things they don't really want to do, that are not to their benefit. Dark pattern techniques currently include questions that trick us into giving an unintended answer; 'Roach Motel' – or getting tangled in an internet process which is hard to escape; 'Privacy Zuckering' where we give up more information about ourselves than we intended (this pattern is named for Facebook's CEO, which probably makes it an issue for the company's Reputation PR team) and 'Confirmshaming: The act of guilting the user into opting into something' (Dark Patterns, 2021).

Impartial reflection is often associated with wisdom. Would interface impartiality be an asset for society in general and not only when engaging with causes or brands? Should we 'proof' ourselves against persuasive interfaces (whether they're well-intentioned or purveyors of dark patterns) by learning to reflect more impartially? Proofing on that scale will not be easy. In 2012 a research team produced a graphical interface to encourage reflection in one particular US State Election, by encouraging more even-handed thought about pros and cons of the election issues. The team proposed that 'while it is difficult to design interfaces for wide public use that subtly nudge people toward a deliberative style of communication, we believe it is possible' (Kriplean et al., 2012, p. 267). Leaving aside that the interface used the 'nudge' in order to achieve the socially desirable objective, the research also reported a reluctance among users to accept data without knowing the communicator's own biases. Another team explored 'Designing for Reflection and Social Persuasion to Promote Sustainable Lifestyles'. The result was 'BinCam', a graphic and text interface and 'social persuasive system to motivate reflection and behavioural change in the food waste and recycling habits of young adults' (Thieme et al., 2012, p. 2337). Interpreting persuasion as 'a purposeful attempt to change a person's attitude or behavior' (Thieme et al., 2012, p. 2338):

> We envisage our work will motivate future HCI research bridging social media and strategies of social persuasion to promote change.
> (Thieme et al., 2012, p. 2346)

Openness seems key to a productive relationship between PR, interfaces and wider publics. Ethically inclined PUIs, including those like BinCam with a message whose virtues can seem unarguable to many, should be open about their own preferences *and communication techniques*. The alternative is to fake objectivity so users will trust slanted content. How to pretend to be objective? Perhaps by presenting a message as a service to society? Putting the word 'Social' in front of a noun like 'Persuasion' is not a solution either, whatever the supposed virtues of either word. Language camouflage has nothing to do with objectivity. 'Social' can signal a bias or conceal one. A full explanation of the persuasive methods used would be more ethical. Transparency and objectivity proclamations, if such a thing is possible in PR, will not be good enough to create an even relationship between the user and a fully persuasive interface. The interface must be clear about its own subjectivities, just as a news release must be clear about the organisation behind it. Persuasive User Interfaces that prime or nudge are not always being open with us, however fluently they speak.

The time for discussing what PR could do with persuasive interfaces is now. PUIs won't be neglected by users or by organisations whose needs may be too complex to ethically codify. Without complete openness and impartial reflection from the interface, the allure of their design and capabilities may be hard for us to resist. They will be too attractive, too knowledgeable. In other words, too persuasive, and when PR starts working with them there will be no going back.

How will we use persuasive interfaces?

Talking interfaces point to a future as a persuasive PR platform and ultimately as PR practitioners. As they develop, they must be allowed into a public sphere filled with competitive communication. It is the same space that PR itself needs and has helped to maintain. Without open access and competition, the interfaces again turn into potentially irresistible propaganda devices.

The types of talking interfaces involved in this have names which are often used interchangeably but it's been shown that each of them has distinct qualities from a PR viewpoint. VUIs provide information or perform simple services; CUIs suggest possible courses of action, and eventually without being asked; PUIs persuade, hook, nudge or lead us towards a preferred course of action on contested subjects. All three can communicate a message, and have some persuasive powers. All three matter to the future of communication: Business to Individual, Government to Individual, Nonprofit to Individual. They will affect the balance of communication between technology and human. Real or pretended power disguised as persuasion is already popular with government departments, celebrities, idealists, realists, campaigners, and corporations. They will all be interested in IUIs that can at least maintain their existing power relations, or strengthen them.

The interfaces involved in this may be called assistants, advisors, and partners (but for now probably not leaders, whether they lead or not). They will encourage and nudge, prime facts with feelings and vice versa, perhaps to push people into getting help or products they need; or into getting policies, help or products they don't need. Aristotle's logos, ethos and pathos will be captured in interface data, tone, design, and sentiment, and in our eternal fascination with technology that will communicate (but not necessarily look) more like us than ever before.

Along with the opportunities, we have suggested that persuasive interfaces could intensify familiar problems. They involve the line between wanting to understand us and continuously monitoring us, and concerns about what happens to our data. It is also possible – and a problem for society as a productive, collective cooperating unit – that some persuasive IUIs might help PR weaken itself in some fields by weakening the environment of competing views that made PR necessary. It could be done by interfaces blending persuasion and compulsion so well that human audiences won't know or want to know if they're being helped or controlled. We may prefer to abolish alternative views or products from our minds and give ourselves over to the superior reasoning powers of interfaces, to the point where a single well-directed word could summon up an entire, intolerant superstructure that cleverly exploits our pre-existing opinions and stereotypes, voluntarily shutting down alternatives in our minds before they can speak for themselves. As usual, novelists, philosophers and historians have raised this possibility well ahead of science and technology. In this way PR could lose one of its redeeming functions by using PUIs to reinforce and strengthen perceptions until something quite subjective feels concrete and true to the target audience and competitive persuasion disappears. Voluntary intellectual imprisonment has been welcomed by humans before without any help from IUIs. Persuasive User Interfaces may take our capacity for self-imprisonment to a new place, one from which it is hard to escape.

Could more open, persuasive IUIs maintain a healthy balance between competing messages, or will it create a civic wasteland, which the philosopher John Stuart Mill in *On Liberty* (1859) famously described as the 'tyranny of opinion' and 'the tyranny of the majority'

(Mill et al., 1977, pp. 201, 272)? Persuasive interfaces raise these questions for PR at the same time as they raise tremendous prospects for a flourishing, imaginative, and inclusive public arena.

References

Apple Siri. (2020). Homepage. Retrieved from https://www.apple.com/siri/

Aristotle & Bartlett, R. C. (2019). *Aristotle's "Art of Rhetoric"*. eBook. Chicago, IL: The University of Chicago Press.

Bohm, D. (1996). *On dialogue*. Abingdon: Routledge.

Chen, G. D., Lee, J. H., Wang, C. Y., Chao, P. Y., Li, L. Y., & Lee, T. Y. (2012). An empathic avatar in a computer-aided learning program to encourage and persuade learners. *Journal of Educational Technology & Society, 15*(2), 62–72.

Dark Patterns. (2021). Types of Dark Pattern. Retrieved from https://www.darkpatterns.org/types-of-dark-pattern

Fogg, B. J. (2002). Persuasive technology: Using computers to change what we think and do. *Ubiquity, 2002* (December), 2.

Fogg, B. J. (2003). *Persuasive technology: Using computers to change what we think and do*. Amsterdam: Morgan Kaufmann.

Google Play. (2020). Homepage. Retrieved from https://play.google.com/store/apps/details?id=com.google.android.apps.googleassistant&hl=en_US&gl=US

Guerini, M., Stock, O., Zancanaro, M., O'Keefe, D. J., Mazzotta, I., de Rosis, F., … & Aylett, R. (2011). Approaches to verbal persuasion in intelligent user interfaces. In P. Petta (Ed.), *Emotion-Oriented Systems* (pp. 559–584). Berlin and Heidelberg: Springer. Retrieved from http://www.dokeefe.net/pub/Guerini&11EOS.pdf

Hoschka, P. (1996). *Computers as assistants: A new generation of support systems*. Mahwah, NJ: Lawrence Erlbaum Associates.

Joo, Y. K., & Lee, J. E. R. (2014). Can "The Voices in the Car" persuade drivers to go green? Effects of benefit appeals from in-vehicle voice agents and the role of drivers' affective states on eco-driving. *Cyberpsychology, Behavior, and Social Networking, 17*(4), 255–261.

Josekutty Thomas, R., Masthoff, J., & Oren, N. (2017, March). Personalising healthy eating messages to age, gender and personality: Using Cialdini's principles and framing. *Proceedings of the 22nd international conference on intelligent user interfaces companion* (pp. 81–84). New York: Association for Computing Machinery.

Kendall, L., Chaudhuri, B., & Bhalla, A. (2020). Understanding technology as situated practice: Everyday use of voice user interfaces among diverse groups of users in urban India. *Information Systems Frontiers, 22*, 585–605.

Kompella, K. (2021). Speech emotion recognition: The next step in the user experience. *Speech Technology, 26*(1), 14–15.

Kriplean, T., Morgan, J., Freelon, D., Borning, A., & Bennett, L. (2012, February). Supporting reflective public thought with considerit. *Proceedings of the ACM 2012 conference on computer supported cooperative work*. NY: New York. Association for Computing Machinery, (pp. 265–274). Retrieved from https://dl.acm.org/doi/pdf/10.1145/2145204.2145249?casa_token=Yco_XHCkSa0AAAAA:_-xT5WFLJQSWymv7COlQ5NaIA_bVYma5J1sIVoPd7a5OGaoehg6IyK0oPA37W0beWGUCEXzEvVAQkn8

Machiavelli, N. (1992). *The prince*. New York: Knopf.

Mazzotta, I., De Rosis, F., & Carofiglio, V. (2007). Portia: A user-adapted persuasion system in the healthy-eating domain. *IEEE Intelligent Systems*, *22*(6), 42–51. Retrieved from http://citeseerx.ist.psu.edu/viewdoc/download?doi=10.1.1.562.4397&rep=rep1&type=pdf

Microsoft Alexa for PC. (2020). Homepage. Retrieved from https://www.microsoft.com/en-us/p/alexa/9n12z3cctcnz?activetab=pivot:overviewtab

Mill, J. S. & Robson, Ann P., & John M. (1977). On liberty. In *The collected works of John Stuart Mill*, Volume XVIII. Kindle Book. Indianapolis, IN: Liberty Fund, Inc. Toronto: University of Toronto. Retrieved from https://oll-resources.s3.us-east-2.amazonaws.com/oll3/store/titles/233/Mill_0223-18_EBk_v6.0.pdf

Moore, R. J., & Arar, R. (2018). Conversation UX design: An introduction. In R. J. Moore; M. H. Szymanski; R. Arar; G. Ren (Eds.), *Studies in conversational UX design* (pp. 1–16). Cham: Springer.

Omnicon Health Group. (2016, December). Voice recognition technology: A basic user interface with advanced capabilities. Retrieved from https://www.omnicomhealthgroup.com/pdfs/VoiceRecognitioninHealthcare.pdf

Orji, R. (2016, April). Persuasion and culture: Individualism-collectivism and susceptibility to influence strategies. In *PPT@ PERSUASIVE* (pp. 30–39). Retrieved from http://ceur-ws.org/Vol-1582/16Orji.pdf

Paay, J., Kjeldskov, J., Papachristos, E., Hansen, K. M., Jørgensen, T., & Overgaard, K. L. (2020). Can digital personal assistants persuade people to exercise? *Behaviour & Information Technology*, 1–17. Retrieved from https://www.tandfonline.com/doi/pdf/10.1080/0144929X.2020.1814412?-casa_token=BVAIjyObzZgAAAAA:-4mDMSEIF8n89VnfT2VtSDOD-F3G0R79__JFthKpl8FEFxZHjPUw3L80PgWFpsvIsi2xLYCEIWwQ9Wg

Payr, S. (2013). Virtual butlers and real people: Styles and practices in long-term use of a companion. In R. Trappl (Ed), *Your virtual butler* (pp. 134–178). Berlin and Heidelberg: Springer. Retrieved from https://www.researchgate.net/profile/Sabine-Payr/publication/262281847_Virtual_Butlers_and_Real_People_Styles_and_Practices_in_Long-Term_Use_of_a_Companion/links/5aafbe37458515ecebea060c/Virtual-Butlers-and-Real-People-Styles-and-Practices-in-Long-Term-Use-of-a-Companion.pdf

Porcheron, M., Fischer, J. E., Reeves, S., & Sharples, S. (2018, April). Voice interfaces in everyday life. *Proceedings of the 2018 CHI conference on human factors in computing systems* (pp. 1–12). Retrieved from https://dl.acm.org/doi/pdf/10.1145/3173574.3174214?casa_token=yF3WrglbbRMAAAAA:-cYC7yGRG3dDpDVnATb4uEuss4A0znoj5emXOHtKmWsGuejQF-KA2A38qNQn9MVDByPcULlwSPaLbxRw

Requejo, D. (2018, April 6). How voice user interface is taking over the world, and why you should care. *Good Rebels*. Retrieved from https://medium.com/@goodrebels/how-voice-user-interface-is-taking-over-the-world-and-why-you-should-care-54474bd56f81

Rolandi, W. (2018). Can we talk? *Speech Technology, 23*(1), 5.

Schulman, D., & Bickmore, T. (2009, April). Persuading users through counseling dialogue with a conversational agent. *Proceedings of the 4th international conference on persuasive technology* (pp. 1–8). New York: Association for Computing Machinery.

Seering, J., Fang, T., Damasco, L., Chen, M. C., Sun, L., & Kaufman, G. (2019, May). Designing user interface elements to improve the quality and civility of discourse in online commenting behaviors. *Proceedings of the 2019 CHI Conference on human factors in computing systems* (pp. 1–14). Retrieved from https://dl.acm.org/doi/pdf/10.1145/3290605.3300836?casa_token=JPzf2jR-trHwAAAAA:YJEWOEWxhbuVALjwHx-AjvkxInAO42Fk5ePFY2iOD-jEZbKZu3KqoHZGDlPqD-mu-rgkbi2u7Pk_GSfw

Shalyminov, I., Dušek, O., & Lemon, O. (2018). Neural response ranking for social conversation: A data-efficient approach. *arXiv preprint arXiv:1811.00967.*

Singh, M. (2018). *Evaluating persuasive user interfaces for online help-seeking for domestic violence* (No. M. Eng (Mechanical)). Deakin University. Retrieved from https://dro.deakin.edu.au/view/DU:30110823

Thieme, A., Comber, R., Miebach, J., Weeden, J., Kraemer, N., Lawson, S., & Olivier, P. (2012, May). "We've bin watching you" designing for reflection and social persuasion to promote sustainable lifestyles. *Proceedings of the SIGCHI conference on human factors in computing systems* (pp. 2337–2346). Retrieved from https://dl.acm.org/doi/pdf/10.1145/2145204.2145249?casa_token=Yco_XHCkSa0AAAAA:_-xT5WFLJQSWymv7COlQ5NaIA_bVY-ma5J1sIVoPd7a5OGaoehg6IyK0oPA37W0beWGUCEXzEvVAQkn8

Thomas, G. (2017, Nov 3). Opinion: the future of voice user interfaces. *Medium*. Retrieved from https://medium.com/bbc-news-labs/the-future-of-vui-36c5105f0846

Toxboe, A. (2020, April 22). 6 persuasive IU design patterns to hook users. *Studio by UXPin*. Retrieved from https://www.uxpin.com/studio/blog/6-persuasive-ui-design-patterns-to-hook-users/

Trappl, R. (Ed). (2013). *Your virtual butler.* Berlin and Heidelberg: Springer-Verlag.

UXPin. (2021). VUI: The future of voice interface design explained. *Studio by UXPin*. Retrieved from https://www.uxpin.com/studio/blog/voice-user-interface/

6   PR and the interface 'face'

Harnessing hyper-personalised persuasion

Towards a 'PR-friendly' IUI personality

The interfaces that we have talked about are PR assets in their own right. They are also essential for putting a complete 'face' on the interface; a personality advanced enough for PR to use. A PR-friendly interface personality is sophisticated (non-binary and capable of nuance). It is adaptable; a good talker and listener; a trusted source of data. It might have strong powers of persuasion; know how to use touch, sight, and voice to influence opinion. It can read our emotions and, for a convincing humanlike personality, express its own 'feelings' to suit the occasion. An interface with personality attracts us because we trust its reliability, usability and convenience. We want to make requests through it, listen to it and confide our feelings to it.

Does any of the personality research throw light on IUI's relationship with PR? Personality-building has preoccupied interface design for some time. More must be done, one voice mail research paper commented in 1996, 'to determine how users could benefit from imaginative personalities' (Chin, 1996, p. 249). 'Imaginative' personalities matter to PR too, because memorable personalities matter. Humans read faces for clues to a personality and the interface is the gateway to personality for an artificial agent and its owners, the biggest influence on a user's 'tendency to attribute mental states to the system' (Parlangeli et al., 2012, p. 1123):

> This tendency, as this study seems to confirm, seems to be a ubiquitous and unavoidable feature of human beings, and possibly one even more complex than what it is generally believed to be.
>
> (Parlangeli et al., 2012, p. 1123)

Creating interface personalities must help the IUI carry out PR functions. One of the first needs is to find a helpful definition of 'personality',

DOI: 10.4324/9781003111320-6

a concept full of variables. Understanding the variables may produce interfaces with characters which are attractive to users, and which can adapt to us.

A workable definition could help interfaces and PR discover which of the many elements of personality 'can be used to influence human perception' in the words of a thesis on conversational agents (Smestad, 2018, p. 7). Some of the systematic, empirical, applied approaches taken so far have avoided the messy, random, multi-layered, emotional and changeable aspects of personality and concentrated on shaping our perceptions of the interface by developing practical design features. In this approach, interface personality relies on 'the look and feel of the site' (Schlecht, 2017). Interface designers work with features already described: micro expressions and eye tracking to assess the feelings of the human using the interface, experiments with colours and music, fitting an interface personality to the expectations of specific groups, applying 'adaptive design' which:

> provides more efficient communication between the interface and the user, increases overall performance and satisfaction, and minimizes the frustration experienced by users.
>
> (Alves et al., 2020, p. 6)

Adaptive interfaces, sensitive to changes in the user, could produce deeper interface personalities that are equally sensitive to PR's needs, although much refinement is needed. It's been suggested that 'adaptive strategies may themselves need to be adapted to the individual traits of their users' (Gajos & Chauncey, 2017, p. 304).

Systems-focused approaches like that are offshoots of 'activity theory', which holds that an activity system embodies, not just the immediate task, but historical, cultural and other influences on the participants. This is an accepted idea in archaeology as well as design and may have extra value for PR practitioners planning interface personalities. Activity theory says that 'The formation of human activity is also the beginning of personality' (Davydov, 1999, p. 39). The beginning of personality, and possibly the beginnings of seeing personality in others. The roots of that connection were persuasively presented in a 2021 investigation of our need for interfaces with personality. It should be quoted in full:

> It may seem that the purpose-oriented participants focus on the functions of AI. Nonetheless, it was noted that such components as tone of voice and humor, traits that reflect human personality characteristics, still arise in participants' discussion of AI.

Arguably this involves a return to the primordial, innate, universal pre-conscious nature of the Jungian concept of archetype. The archetypes are components of the collective unconscious and, therefore, a longing for human association in inanimate objects remains present even if hidden and unrealized.

(Karimova & Goby, 2021, p. 235)

Activity theory also suggests that the easier something is to understand and use, the more it will be used, or consumed. That idea too has been applied to interfaces:

As human capital becomes associated with one specific interface, consumers become loyal to that interface because switching to a competitor would cost the consumer time in acquiring new competitor-specific skills.

(Murray, 2004, p. 4)

A full interface personality needs emotion, which we talked about in Chapter 3, and research works with definitions strategic communicators would find familiar. In one case a computer model was created with reactive, stable and active (or short-term) personalities, which are triggered when responding to daily weather patterns (van der Heider & Trivino, 2010). Automotive voice assistants have been given two dimensions of casual to formal, and equivalent to subordinate, with four optimal 'personalities' of a friend of the human driver, an admirer, the 'aunt (supportive and close)', and the 'butler (at your service)' (Braun et al., 2019). Another interesting analysis of Alexa, Siri, Google Assistant and Microsoft Cortana used measures of low to high warmth and competence. The spontaneous human qualities that produce a warm personality are one reason why 'Google is tapping creative writers from Pixar and The Onion [a satirical news platform] to infuse personality into Assistant's responses in hopes of creating an emotional bond between users and the IPA' (Lopatovska, 2020, p. 336), incidentally suggesting that Google thinks 'the future of our technology will be intrinsically conversational' (Dye, 2016). A Postgraduate study of chatbots took a fourfold approach to personality that PR might also use whenever it communicates reputation with interfaces in general:

1   The brand mission, goals and values
2   A deep understanding of the users and their needs
3   The role/job of the chatbot
4   An appropriate personality model

(Smestad, 2018, p. 18)

Other research, including research on interfaces, concentrates on the 'Big Five' personality traits (Conscientiousness, Extraversion, Agreeableness, Neuroticism, Openness) (see, for example, Lee et al., 2019). The Big Five may 'contain too many dimensions to be practicable foundations for many design use cases' (Braun & Alt, 2020, p. 123). It has not realised its full potential in PR, which usually works with large numbers of people grouped by interests rather than personality traits, but it enters the shared orbit of interface design and PR when strategic communication needs an interface to persuade users as individuals. Research has after all found that 'users performed better when they handled an interface that matched their personality type' (Alves et al., 2020, p. 5) (see also Kostov & Fukuda, 2001, p. 1128).

The development of IUI personality (or rather personalities) and all the other interface assets we've looked at are going to matter to PR. A convincing interface personality would present PR with new possibilities and obligations. It raises issues for everyone (whether or not they're interested in communication strategy) to think about even if they can't be satisfactorily resolved, except by pressure of time and events. It's useful to return to the questions asked at the start of this exploration of PR's future with intelligent user interfaces.

What do IUIs mean for PR?

We have asked what intelligent user interfaces are and how they could affect PR. At the moment, interfaces are what we use to obtain services, usually in exchange for information about users. What are interfaces trying to do? At the moment, user interfaces provide a place for users to command a machine and to get information and services from the machine. They are often presented by their developers as helpers or tools if we are in education or have particular physical or health needs. In the home they help us listen to music, turn the lights off, watch who comes to our front door. They help artificial agents and human beings encounter the world together, whether on military missions or cooking dinner.

We've seen that the role of interfaces as a tool is changing, and because of communication. 'In previous styles of interaction between people and machines, the human acted as an operator of the machine. 'However, in the case of computerised tasks, humans do not operate the computer, they communicate with it to accomplish a task' investigators advised in 1995 (Richter & Salvendy, 1995, p. 281). The relationship between IUIs and humans depends on a communication relationship, capable of operating at a personal and also public level.

No one in PR should ignore interfaces. They are getting more interesting to users, thanks to research into the 'human factors' that best help interface usability. IUIs are becoming more conversational and observant. They are learning more about us. They are beginning to learn about communicating ideas. They will learn how to work in partnership with us. We will learn to trust them with more of our lives, which means trusting the owners of the interface – the brands or products or campaigners or authorities who are embodied in the interface's 'personality'. How should PR start to think about IUIs like that?

The first step is to repeat the need for PR to understand that the interface has an authority and a message of its own. Interfaces are becoming recipients and shapers of perceptions. Perhaps the biggest mistake of all, which would have consequences for society, would be for PR to not notice the interface just when its 'invisible influence' is growing. For that reason IUIs must be visible when they are involved in strategic communication. Their methods and independent influence must be understood. The impact of IUIs on society will be much deeper than the daily shocks to public communication delivered by social media. All systems, whether social systems in the real world or social media in the virtual world often adopt similar implicit biases from their developers or the cases they learned from and these biases will be made more explicit through IUIs.

At the moment, PR is unprepared for the more personal relationships IUIs will develop with target audiences. Others are preparing, in October, 2020 the US government's Defense Advanced Research Projects Agency (DARPA) posted a call for projects related to 'Influence Campaign Awareness and Sensemaking' (INCA):

> The US is engaged with its adversaries in an asymmetric, continual, adaptive war of weaponized influence narratives. Adversaries exploit misinformation and true information delivered via influence messaging: blogs, tweets, and other online multimedia content. Analysts require effective tools for continual sensemaking of the vast, noisy, adaptive information environment to identify adversary influence campaigns.
>
> (DARPA, 2020)

To some extent that account describes the whole public communication space and all its occupants, whether or not we agree with the activities of particular governments, non-profits, companies and individuals. As they enter this unstable space, IUIs will test the creativity and the conscience of every strategic communicator. For now, their cumulative impact remains unknown. There will be many surprises. We have attempted to present some possibilities.

To return to an earlier question: how could PR change? It will probably continue as a distinct practice, since enhancing and organising what we want to say is human nature. Once again, we remember the historically incontrovertible fact, opportunity and threat raised in Chapter 1: 'Man has developed extensions for practically everything he used to do with his body' (McLuhan & Gordon, 2011, p. 4). With IUIs, the process is accelerated. The latest extension of faculties once confined to our bodies is underway, and with brain-computer interfaces, haptics and conversation interfaces IUIs may extend whatever they represent or have to say into us. IUIs are not the end of managed public communication. They do mark the start of a much stronger communication relationship with technology, taking us closer to connecting with them as a partner and almost as a fellow-human. We all need to think about what this means for strategic communication. It isn't going to go away. It is happening, and it is worth making the obvious point here that so far in human history technologically advancing civil societies have not functioned without close connections to activities that today happen to be collected under the name of 'public relations'.

There are good reasons to be optimistic about PR's place in society, for the second step is for PR to listen to the human identities about to enter the public space in force, thanks to IUIs. This may be one of the great episodes of human empowerment, and maybe of liberation. Consider again the experiences that interfaces delivering touch, talk or VR could offer to the severely disabled, lonely and housebound. New voices and views will be heard, new dialogues created, new demands will be made for products and policies. New human and machine influencers will rise out of the new publics, using IUIs creatively to build followers and enter more completely into the communication life of the world. New PR demands and chances will be created for organisations of all kinds. PR will learn to communicate with new identities. The communication capacities of our senses will be enhanced and extended. Thanks to their ability to enlarge the scope of our human faculties, intelligent user interfaces could enrich traditional liberal democracy which at its best, the philosopher Ortega y Gasset (1883–1955) wrote in the dangerous years between the world wars 'carries to the extreme the determination to have consideration for one's neighbor' (Ortega, 1957, p. 56). It is:

> The supreme form of generosity; it is the right which the majority concedes to the minorities and hence it is the noblest cry that has ever resounded in this planet.
>
> (Ortega, 1957, p. 56)

As well as more participation, opinions and audiences, interfaces in the public sphere will stimulate creativity in public relations. IUIs will show strategic communication how to deliver richer experiences of a point of view, product, issue, celebrity, or organisation. Audiences could be drawn into the spirit of a message with haptics, natural language, brain-computer interfaces, adaptive technologies and active listening. PR will deploy these assets for its clients, bringing organisations into vibrant virtual worlds perhaps with their own economies, and show them unexpected publics with valuable identities and interests to contribute.

In the longer term, PR-abled IUIs might be needed to persuade other interfaces, introducing machine to machine (M2M) persuasion into a PR campaign, maybe to influence views on a social trend or breaking crisis, turning the interface itself into a PR-managed influencer. An early version of this is apparent right now with so many of us getting our 'news' and other information on social networks. Our 'trust transference' into new forms of media has encouraged the development social bots spreading what has been called 'low-credibility content' (Shao et al., 2018), as 'actors in online social networks that surreptitiously aim to manipulate public discourse and influence human opinions and behavior in an opaque fashion' (Yang et al., 2019, p. 48). Their potential uses, said the US Department of Homeland Security, 'for good and malicious purposes, are ever expanding' (DHS, 2018). The bots are responding to our suspicions, learning to slow down and spread information in a more 'human' way by imitating human patterns of behaviour. Social bots are one reason why M2M PR may become a very volatile and necessary activity. Far from contemplating extinction, PR may be busier than ever; operating in a more fluid environment, constantly adjusting messages and identities to shifting perceptions. The fact that bots need not be controlled and coordinated, and can act on their own, or with humans, suggests that PR may itself become far more collaborative, encouraging co-ownership of an organisation's public identity with human audiences, bots or popular independent interfaces. That shared sense of 'ownership', as we suggested in Chapter 1, could be important in resolving a crisis, or remaking the public identity of a politician or a celebrity – which may need to happen more often in a world where the interface can be an audience, a medium and a PR consultant at the same time.

IUIs could change public diplomacy: the task of globally communicating perceptions of a government or country. There will be vivid ways to tell the story of a culture or policy. Would it be wise for a democratic government to neglect natural language, haptics or brain-computer interfaces, and leave them to other governments, other regimes? Like nature, PR abhors a vacuum. We again suggest that without competitive public relations, society is vulnerable to manipulative monopolies of opinion. IUIs must be available for all kinds of PR. We won't always like the results. Open-mindedness might be the biggest test that PR-abled IUIs will present to us, because many of them will want to reinforce our feelings or opinions and far more powerfully than social media. Imagine a lifetime of flattery or reinforcement. Never being questioned, but always being steered. Imagine the public sphere becoming a 'people farm' where citizens are observed and herded by interfaces using facts and feeling that are finely tuned to personal preferences.

Should governments regulate PR's adoption of IUIs? Try to understand interfaces as semi-autonomous devices with PR power and not just as medical, financial, educational or military tools? Most recently, in April 2021 the European Commission produced a proposal for an Artificial Intelligence Act, harmonising rules across the bloc with the official goal of making them 'human centric', 'so that people can trust that the technology is used in a way that is safe and compliant with the law, including the respect of fundamental rights' (European Commission, 2021, p. 1). Proposals include setting up risk management systems (p. 44); formalising human oversight (p. 51); establishing 'notifying authorities' in the member states (p. 58); a certification process for 'high risk' AI systems (p. 65); 'AI regulatory sandboxes' to reduce the burden on small businesses (p. 69); 'transparency obligations' requiring AI systems to tell 'natural persons' when they are interacting with it (p. 69); a Europe-wide Artificial Intelligence Board (p. 72); enforcement, codes of conduct and penalties (pp. 76, 80, 81) and a general desire to 'help shape global norms' (p. 5).

Less scrupulous PR practitioners might not welcome the transparency obligations, but even if strategic communication was included in AI legislation, for instance to mitigate its impact on human emotion, could well-intentioned and less well-intentioned governments worldwide agree how to enforce it? How long would it be before the limits of that agreement are tested, advantages taken, exceptions made, boundaries stretched, and finally broken? How much government infrastructure would be needed to keep up with the interface revolution? Attractive platforms that can shape our perception usually outgrow whatever function they were originally designed to perform. Our fascination with new media can't be confined. We see fresh possibilities and escape old limits. The rise of IUIs may show once again that PR's influence on the tools it uses, and vice versa, cannot easily be checked.

IUIs will change PR's activities and operational assumptions. IUIs will not change the reasons why PR is an actor in society, or fundamentally how it operates. Shannon's Mathematical Theory of Communication outlined in Chapter 1 will continue to underpin PR's work. Moreover, the changing activities won't happen all at once. PR practitioners will reject some IUIs as ineffective, and won't at first know what to do with the effective ones. Other IUIs may start their PR career by being treated as amusements, much like the early moving pictures, the telephone and many other world-changing technologies. This attitude is at least as old as the steam powered devices made by Hero of Alexandria in the first century AD, which were also viewed as novelties. But the trajectory and velocity of interface developments means PR shouldn't have to wait too long to see their true potential and meaning. Not as long, say, as travellers waited for the Kitty Hawk to morph into passenger jets. Perhaps not even as long as the time between the invention of the Internet and its take-up by PR. This book is about the medium-term future awaiting public relations. In the long term the biggest question is whether PR is human-led or managed and controlled by artificial agents with their own M2M interfaces, and what we think about that. Stephen Hawking is among the many prominent scientists and AI pioneers who have urged us to think carefully about what artificial intelligence might do for and to humanity. PR's part in this is to reflect on the 'face' of AI – the intelligent user interface. The intelligent interface confronts us with the possibility of a subordinate human role in PR, one of the most human-centred of all human activities. That possibility may seem unlikely today. It is an open question for tomorrow.

References

Alves, T., Natálio, J., Henriques-Calado, J., & Gama, S. (2020). Incorporating personality in user interface design: A review. *Personality and Individual Differences, 155*, 109709.

Bernays, E. L. (2005). *Propaganda: With an introduction by Mark Crispin Miller.* New York: Ig.

Braun, M., & Alt, F. (2020). Identifying personality dimensions for characters of digital agents. In B. A. El, Y. Abdelrahman, & S. Abdennadher (Eds.), *Character computing* (pp. 123–137). Cham: Springer. Retrieved from http://www.medien.ifi.lmu.de/pubdb/publications/pub/braun2020character/braun2020character.pdf

Braun, M., Mainz, A., Chadowitz, R., Pfleging, B., & Alt, F. (2019, May). At your service: Designing voice assistant personalities to improve automotive user interfaces. *Proceedings of the 2019 CHI conference on human factors in computing systems* (pp. 1–11). New York: Association for Computing Machinery.

Chin, J. P. (1996, April). Personality trait attributions to voice mail user interfaces. *Conference companion on human factors in computing systems* (pp. 248–249). New York: Association for Computing Machinery.

DARPA. (2020). Influence Campaign Awareness and Sensemaking (IN-CAS). Presolicitation. *Beta.SAM.gov.* Retrieved from https://beta.sam.gov/opp/6bbca26d91df4eff96b4edfa2386c35f/view#general

Davydov, V. V. (1999). The content and unsolved problems of activity theory. *Perspectives on Activity Theory, 1*, 39–52.

DHS. (2018, May). *Social media bots overview.* National Protection and Programs Directorate. Retrieved from https://niccs.cisa.gov/sites/default/files/documents/pdf/ncsam_socialmediabotsoverview_508.pdf?trackDocs=ncsam_socialmediabotsoverview_508.pdf

Dye, J. (2016, October 10). How the onion and pixar helped build google assistant. *Android Authority.* Retrieved from https://www.androidauthority.com/google-assistant-onion-pixar-721227/

European Commission. (2021, April 21). *Laying down harmonised rules on Artificial Intelligence (Artificial Intelligence Act) and amending certain Union legislative acts.* Proposal for a regulation of the European Parliament and of the Council. COM (2021) 206 final. 2021/0106(COD). Luxembourg: Office for Official Publications of the European Communities. Retrieved from https://eur-lex.europa.eu/legal-content/EN/TXT/?uri=CELLAR%3Ae0649735-a372-11eb-9585-01aa75ed71a1

Gajos, K. Z., & Chauncey, K. (2017, March). The influence of personality traits and cognitive load on the use of adaptive user interfaces. *Proceedings of the 22nd international conference on intelligent user interfaces* (pp. 301–306). New York: Association for Computing Machinery.

Karimova, G. Z., & Goby, V. P. (2020). The adaptation of anthropomorphism and archetypes for marketing artificial intelligence. *Journal of Consumer Marketing, 38*(2), 229–238.

Kostov, V., & Fukuda, S. (2001, September). Development of man-machine interfaces based on user preferences. *Proceedings of the 2001 IEEE international conference on control applications (CCA'01)(Cat. No. 01CH37204)* (pp. 1124–1128). Piscataway, NJ: IEEE.

Lee, S. Y., Lee, G., Kim, S., & Lee, J. (2019). Expressing personalities of conversational agents through visual and verbal feedback. *Electronics, 8*(7), 794.

Lopatovska, I. (2020). Personality dimensions of intelligent personal assistants. *Proceedings of the 2020 conference on human information interaction and retrieval* (pp. 333–337). New York: Association for Computing Machinery. Retrieved from https://dl.acm.org/doi/pdf/10.1145/3343413.3377993?casa_token=PwJqz_uTK7gAAAAA:NSPY9LZJR3Ph8akLGVgIh8QcxvAGm_vPa1ABHpXGq_Ij6lbUHASVATQa9IP8tOLtoHRVtEvnwdUl

McLuhan, M., & Gordon, W. T. (2011). *The Gutenberg galaxy: The making of typographic man.* eBook. Toronto: University of Toronto Press.

Murray, K. B. (2004). *The role of skill-based habits of use in consumer choice* (Doctoral dissertation, University of Alberta).

Ortega, G. J. (1957). *The revolt of the masses: Authorized translation from the Spanish.* New York: W.W. Norton.

Parlangeli, O., Chiantini, T., & Guidi, S. (2012). A mind in a disk: The attribution of mental states to technological systems. *Work, 41*(Supplement 1), 1118–1123.

Richter, L. A., & Salvendy, G. (1995). Effects of personality and task strength on performance in computerized tasks. *Ergonomics,* 38(2), 281–291.

Schlecht, D. (2017, October 9). These are the 5 big differences between UX and UI design. *Career Foundry.* Retrieved from https://careerfoundry.com/en/blog/ux-design/5-big-differences-between-ux-and-ui-design/

Shao, C., Ciampaglia, G. L., Varol, O., Yang, K. C., Flammini, A., & Menczer, F. (2018). The spread of low-credibility content by social bots. *Nature Communications,* 9(1), 1–9.

Smestad, T. L. (2018). *Personality matters! Improving the user experience of chatbot interfaces-personality provides a stable pattern to guide the design and behaviour of conversational agents* (Master's thesis, NTNU).

van der Heide, A., & Trivino, G. (2010, July). Simulating emotional personality in human computer interfaces. In *International conference on fuzzy systems* (pp. 1–7). IEEE. Retrieved from http://www.avdheide.nl/publications/VanderHeide_Trivino_[2010]_Simulating_Emotional_Personality_in_Human_Computer_Interfaces.pdf

Yang, K. C., Varol, O., Davis, C. A., Ferrara, E., Flammini, A., & Menczer, F. (2019). Arming the public with artificial intelligence to counter social bots. *Human Behavior and Emerging Technologies, 1*(1), 48–61. Retrieved from https://onlinelibrary.wiley.com/doi/pdfdirect/10.1002/hbe2.115

Index

For Product Safety Concerns and Information please contact our EU representative GPSR@taylorandfrancis.com Taylor & Francis Verlag GmbH, Kaufingerstraße 24, 80331 München, Germany